THE BOOK OF
Spells

THE BOOK OF
Spells

A treasury of
spells, rituals, and blessings

Marie Bruce

SIRIUS

All images courtesy of Shutterstock

SIRIUS

This edition published in 2023 by Sirius Publishing, a division of
Arcturus Publishing Limited,
26/27 Bickels Yard, 151–153 Bermondsey Street,
London SE1 3HA

ISBN: 978-1-3988-2757-8
AD011030UK

Printed in China

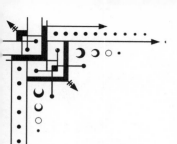

CONTENTS

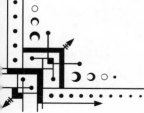

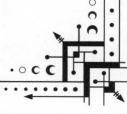

INTRODUCTION

SIT FOR A SPELL...

Spell books have been around for centuries, and most witches have at least one volume that they reach for in times of crisis. In Wiccan circles, the spell book is known as the Book of Shadows, or BOS. In other circles, it is called a grimoire. Whatever its name, the spell book is a vital tool for magical practitioners, providing information, instruction, comfort, and a sense of control when life gets messy.

Many practitioners like to create their own spell books, writing out their tried and trusted spells and rituals in a private journal. This is a good way to bring together all the spells that have worked especially well for you, so that you have them all in one place.

Other practitioners prefer to work entirely from published books of spells, such as this one. These books can be a great time-saving device, as they tend to hold spells for all purposes and are easy to use. Of course, spells can always be adapted, or used to inspire the practitioner to write their own original spells, so there is more than one way to use a book like this one.

In *The Book of Spells,* I have drawn together spells, rituals, blessings, and so on to suit a variety of circumstances. My intention is that this book will become a trusted resource, one that you reach for whenever you need a little magical assistance to make life run more smoothly.

All the spells use easily sourced ingredients and the standard tools of magic, such as the pentacle, athame, etc (see pages 38-9).

This book is for those who are tired of being buffeted by life and who want to steer their own course. It is for people who are fed up with feeling powerless and want to feel powerful instead. It is for those who are looking for a life-enhancing way to develop personal autonomy, achieve goals, and bring about a harmonious and successful life.

This, then, is my gift to you: a comprehensive Book of Shadows with which you can navigate the ups and downs of life. So sit for a spell as we dive into the fascinating world of witchery and spell-craft. Your magical journey is about to begin.

Blessed be,
Marie Bruce

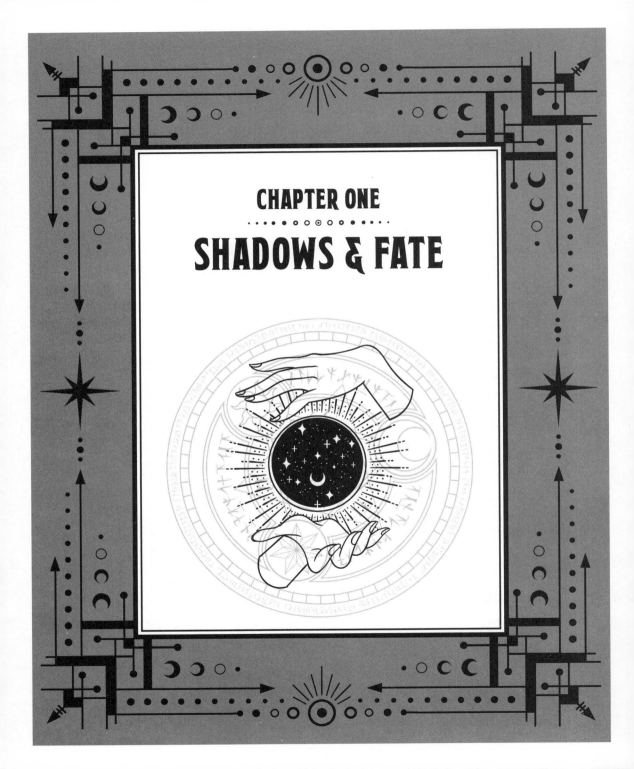

CHAPTER ONE

SHADOWS & FATE

The image of a witch poring over a tome of spells is an enduring one, and it's not far from the truth. Most witches keep spell books, and study their craft voraciously. However, today's witches are a far cry from the stereotypical hags. Witchcraft is a gentle practice that honors nature and respects all forms of life.

Spell-casting is an art form and an intrinsic part of witchery. It takes time to learn but, as with any craft, practice makes perfect. Given time, you will be able to whip up a spell in a few moments, once you have learned how magical correspondences work and which phases of the moon are best for which types of magic.

To begin with, though, we all had to learn the basics. Magic is something that requires commitment and attention to detail. It must be approached with respect and reverence, for you are tapping into universal energies of great power and potential. Applying knowledge with reverence is the key to making effective magic and changing your life for the better using spell-craft.

THE NEOPHYTE WITCH

A neophyte witch is a trainee magical practitioner. Neophyte witches tend to immerse themselves in a period of intense study and spell-craft. Gradually, they learn how to tap into, direct, and release their inner magic, bringing about positive change. This first level of magical training often involves an initiation. It could be a formal initiation into a coven, a self-initiation ritual, or perhaps a life-centered initiation brought about through the catalyst of change or chaos and also known as a baptism of fire.

This does not mean that any prior magical knowledge you have is useless. On the contrary: previous magical training will provide a great foundation. What it does mean is that we must all return to the humble state of novice from time to time, for life is a series of lessons. Approach the teachings of this book with an open mind and the fresh outlook of the novice, regardless of magical experience, because there is always something new to learn if we are open to it.

Living a magical life requires the practitioner to turn inward, exploring motivations and limitations, and delving into the deeper reaches of the mind to find where your strengths and magical talents lie. By finding out who you are on the inside, you will be in a better position to craft a future that helps you thrive, rather than creating the kind of life that is fashionable but leaves you unfulfilled. Use spell-craft to meet your true needs, not to keep up with trends. That way, you will glean the most benefit from your magical skills.

TALL POPPIES

Witches tend to stand out in a crowd because they get things done and make things happen. They are active participants in their own lives and in society. Everyone has an inner power and a strength of will that they can tap into, but lots of people don't use it. Instead, they live in a state of apathy and complaint. This passive indifference toward life is a personal choice, not an inability.

Witches take a different approach, prioritizing personal responsibility and willpower to change their lives for the better. If we don't like something, we change it, or we change our attitude toward it. Witches cast spells and perform rituals. Because of this, they are tuned in to their sense of empowerment. This positive force is what strengthens a witch, enabling them to take life's hard knocks and bounce back.

Having a deep connection with their personal power also means that witches tend to achieve their goals and ambitions, and make their dreams come true. Eventually, people will start to notice this and might even ask you how you always get what you want. Witches are like tall poppies, and someone may try to cut you down to size. However, your ability to bounce back will ensure that you continue to succeed in spite of them.

WHAT IS A SPELL?

A spell or magic ritual is the ability to influence events using willpower and the powers of the natural world. It is a technique used by witches to facilitate an outcome or to bring into being the desire of the witch. Magic is neither black nor white. It is simply energy directed toward an intention. Whether that intention is for good or ill is up to the individual witch, but the power of spell-craft is always neutral.

I have often described spell-casting as *"prayer with props,"* because that is essentially what it is. We use tools such as candles, incense, incantations, written intentions, crystals, plants, and so on, to help us maintain our focus and to bring in aspects of the natural energies with which we work.

Spell-casting is a collaboration between you and the universe, and you have to practice in alignment with the universal tides in order to cast an effective spell or ritual. Many spells incorporate an incantation—words spoken out loud. Sometimes the incantation takes the form of a repetitive chant or a song. Its purpose is to state the intention of the spell.

HOW DO SPELLS WORK?

Spells work by attracting your intention toward you, using the magnetic fields of the universe. Think of the universe as a huge mirror designed to reflect your intentions back at you. This means that what you focus on is what you get. Keeping your thoughts positive will bring good things into your life, while allowing your thoughts to become negative will attract things for you to complain about.

To make positive and effective magic, it is important to have a clear intention and a positive attitude toward the outcome. You must expect good things to come to you, and in a good way. This keeps your personal vibration on a high frequency, which results in positive manifestation of your intentions. Doubting that your magic will work, or being skeptical about magic in general, can delay the outcome, or even sabotage it. You cannot fool the mirror of the universe, and it will always reflect back

the attitude you hold in your heart and mind, so stay positive.

MODERN MAGIC

Over the past few years, magic has had something of a face lift, and has made its way into the mainstream, rebranded in turn as cosmic ordering, the law of attraction, or the manifestation technique. Call it whatever you wish; all these techniques are basically the same thing. They are ways to connect with the power, or magic, of the universe in order to bring about a desired outcome.

If you are already familiar with the law of attraction, then you will have an idea of how magic works. Try to incorporate the law of attraction in your spell-craft to give yourself the best chance of success. Use affirmations, visualizations, vision boarding, and so on as a backup to your spells, and vice versa.

Other spells are designed to be cast daily or weekly. Protection spells, for instance, are cast on a regular basis to keep the magical boundary they create as strong as possible. This is also true for spells for good health or positive family relations. If you are casting to *maintain* something, you will also need to maintain the magic with regular spell work. Most witches cast some kind of simple spell every week. Not only does this maintain the level of magic that surrounds them on a daily basis, it also keeps their skills sharp. Skills can fade, and magic is no exception. As with anything else, regular practice will keep your abilities honed to a high degree.

But spells don't have to be complicated. Since life is so busy for many people, simple spells can sometimes be the best option. The main thing to remember is that magic is cast regularly to keep the good vibes flowing into your life and minimize negative events.

That way, you are surrounding yourself with positive intentions, and your spells should manifest more quickly as a result. The magic of the universe is real, and you can experience it for yourself whenever you choose to tap into it. Spells and rituals are a traditional route to this power, but the modern manifestation paths work too. Using both of these techniques will make your witchery a force to be reckoned with.

MAGIC TAKES WORK

Although movies and TV shows would have us believe that magic is simply a wave of the wand and any dream will come true, in reality magic takes work. If you are casting for a big goal, one spell might not be enough. You will need to layer up the magic by working several spells over a period of time.

BACK UP YOUR SPELLS

You must always be prepared to back up your spells in the mundane world. You can't expect magic to do all the work for you. As I said before, witches are not passive; they are active participants in their own lives, which means that for every spell they cast, they will take action in the real world to help the magic manifest.

What does this mean in practice? It means that if you are casting spells for financial freedom, you will need to stop racking up debt. It means that if you cast for a new job, you need to apply for positions and brush up on your interview skills; if you are casting for love, you need to be open to meeting new people.

Every time you cast a spell, ask yourself how you are going to support the magic in the mundane world. Do you need to make a phone call, send an email, apply for a new job, stop spending on frivolous things, join a club, book a trip? What can you do that will show the universe that you're serious about your goal and that you're willing to put yourself out there, along with your magic?

THE WHEEL OF FORTUNE

The Wheel of Fortune is at work in all our lives, all the time. You are either on your way up or on your way back down, but it is a pattern that is clearly felt by all of us. It is constantly turning, allowing each of us to experience the highs and lows of life.

The Wheel of Fortune is like a cosmic big wheel. For someone to enjoy the view at the top, someone else has to be at the bottom. With each cycle the Wheel draws you higher and higher, until it is your turn at the top; then, inevitably, it begins its descent, taking you back down to earth again. You will know which half of the cycle you are on by noticing the main events of your life in recent months or years.

An upwardly mobile cycle brings promotions, great experiences, new lovers and friends, opportunities, abundance, nice vacations, and all the good things life has to offer. In this stage of the cycle, it will seem as if everything is just coming to you, as you realize your dreams and enjoy life to the full.

A downward cycle, however, tends to strip things away from you, so you experience bereavements, divorce, job loss, poverty, rifts with family and friends, etc. It can be frustrating and debilitating. But the Wheel of Fortune doesn't take away anything you were meant to keep; it removes that which has been holding you back or has served its purpose. When you are on a downward cycle, it can feel as if your life has been emptied out completely, and there is nothing left but the void of what used to be. But take heart, because when you feel that you are at your lowest ebb, that is a sign that you have reached the bottom of the Wheel and the worst is over.

What does the Wheel of Fortune have to do with spell-casting? Quite a lot, actually, because once you have identified how the Wheel is turning right now, you can use the right kinds of spells to reap the most benefit from the journey. So if you are on the upward cycle, use spells to ensure that the Wheel of Fortune brings you the opportunities and things you really want. If you are on a downward cycle, use damage-limitation and healing spells to make the process easier to deal with.

It must also be said that many people come to magic through a sense of sheer desperation, when life is going wrong for them and they don't know which way to turn. For people in such situations, magic seems like their last hope, and frequently becomes a new way of life, as they begin to harness their inner power and make positive changes in their lives.

However you found this path and this book, whether you are in dire straits or a seasoned practitioner, know that you are welcome here and that for the time being, we share this magical journey together.

UNIVERSAL TIDES

Just as the Wheel of Fortune governs the patterns of your personal life, the universe is governed by tides of its own. Like the sea tides, the universal tides ebb and flow, and are made up of pure energy. It is these waves that bring the manifestation of your spell.

Have you ever noticed that sometimes lots of great things just come to you, all at once? It could be a raise, a promotion, a new lover, a pet etc. Because like attracts like, when good things are snowballing into your life it means that the universal tides are coming in. If you are in the habit of casting spells, this is when they will start to manifest or, as the saying goes, this is when your ship will come in.

When the universal tide is out, however, you are more likely to notice how quiet things are, because this is a fallow period of rest. It is a good time to determine what you want to focus on next and begin casting for those goals. The results might not manifest in the very next incoming tide, but at some point, the tides will bring your desire to you.

Witches learn to keep track of shifts in the energy around them, and they know how to tap into these shifts for a higher purpose. Keeping a journal is a good way to identify the energies around you, and to see how and when your goals manifest. Track when something good happens, or when you have experienced a loss. That way you get to know how the tides of life influence the events of your life, and you can learn to work with them in your spells and rituals, knowing that you will be working *with* nature, not against her.

A PROCESS OF ENLIGHTENMENT

Magic is a journey toward enlightenment. It will teach you that there is far more to the world than you imagined. When you step onto the magical path, you may be skeptical, and this is understandable. A certain amount of skepticism is healthy, because it keeps you from being gullible. As you start to see your goals manifest, however, you will find that your belief in magic grows stronger, and the stronger your belief, the more powerful your spells will be.

The first time a spell manifests, it can come as a shock. You might be surprised that you have the power to alter the course of your life. The power you are working with is directed by you, so as long as your intentions are good, there is no need to worry that you have unleashed something that cannot be controlled. Enjoy the success of your magic!

That said, it can be tempting to start casting spells for everything, including things you can just as easily achieve without magical assistance. It is important not to take advantage of the universal power, because that will stop the flow of magic. Before you cast a spell, ask yourself if it is absolutely necessary, or if you can achieve this goal on your own. Be sensible with what you cast for. Magic is not an excuse for laziness.

CHAPTER TWO

SECRETS OF SORCERY

Magic has been around for centuries, although we might not always see it as such. Many of the things we take for granted and understand, such as modern medicine or the laws of chemistry, would have been viewed as feats of magic or alchemy in the past. Times change, superstitions are proven to be unfounded, and our understanding of the world develops. We only need to think of technology to see how fast our world is changing. So things that people once viewed as magic are now part of our everyday lives.

What hasn't changed, however, is the human need to believe in powers greater than ourselves, our quest for knowledge and for a deeper understanding of the world. When you stop and think about it, it *is* miraculous that spring comes around every year, or that there is a vast universe out there that we know little about. All of this is magical. All of it is enchanting. And for witches, it is all source material for spell-casting.

Why do witches cast spells? Well, there are lots of reasons, but the main one is that it gives us a sense of personal power and control over our lives. It is also a way to help others. It can be a great comfort to light a candle and say a few words when a loved one is ill and you are feeling helpless. It can be a source of strength to cast protection spells around your property when there has been a spate of burglaries in the area. It can be a healing experience to practice self-love and recover from a broken heart, or a great relief to hear the cat meowing at the door shortly after you have cast a safe-return spell.

To put it in the simplest of terms, casting spells can make you feel better. It makes you feel as if you've done something to address whatever situation you find yourself in— and you have! Spell-casting is a powerful technique, one that even many orthodox religions use, although they would never refer to it as magic. Have you ever gone into a church and been invited to light a candle for someone? This is spell-craft known by another name: prayer. Essentially, it is one and the same, and that is asking for help from a greater power.

Becoming adept at spells and rituals means you need never feel helpless again, because there is always something you can do. Even in the worst of times, such as bereavement, you can cast for strength and healing. There is nothing that cannot be improved with a little sprinkling of magic, no sticky situation that cannot benefit from a spell to smooth it out. So why wouldn't you want to make magic in your life, knowing that, in turn, life will become more magical?

SERENDIPITY AND COINCIDENCE

When magic is afoot there is no such thing as coincidence, because magic works by coming along the path of least resistance. This means that the magic will manifest in the easiest way possible. So if you are casting for a new job, it could be that you hear of a position from a friend or family member, who puts in a good word for you. It also means that you are more likely to trust the outcome of the magic when it manifests in your life, because it has come via a path that is familiar to you, i.e. someone you know.

Rarely does magic show up accompanied by bells and whistles. It's more of a "blink and you'll miss it" scenario. Although occasionally it does arrive with a bang, it is more usual for spells to manifest in quite a routine way. It could be a while before you realize that your spell has worked and you got exactly what you wanted, but it came in such a mundane way that you didn't immediately correlate the results to the spell. This is a natural oversight, especially if you are new to magic.

It might be that you have noticed many more coincidences happening around you since you started to practice spell-craft. Again, this is a sign that the magic is working. It is important not to dismiss such coincidences, because you might inadvertently sabotage the spells you've been casting. When coincidences keep happening, it is because you are attracting the things you need with your own magnetic field. Accept these coincidences graciously and be ready to welcome more of them.

Serendipity is also a feature of a magical life. This is when a series of chance events lead to a happy ending. It is a sudden change in fortune for the better, or a run of good luck. While coincidence is linked to circumstances and situations, serendipity usually links to people, so think chance encounters, and bumping into people at the right time. Serendipity is about networking and building a team, so introductions, interviews, invitations and so on are all at play here.

Again, try not to dismiss these encounters, because they have been brought about for a reason. Of course, you should keep your safety in mind, but try not to reject people out of habit; you could be rejecting the results of your spells! Serendipity is a little louder than coincidence, and has a habit of dropping the right people into your life, seemingly out of the blue, right when you need them most. Magical meetings feel different from mundane ones, so trust your intuition and see where these new acquaintances take you. Trust that these people have come into your life for a good reason, and vice versa—they might need you just as much as you need them.

WHEN SOMEONE ELSE GETS WHAT YOU WANT

Another clear sign that you are heading in the right direction with your magical endeavors is when someone close to you gets exactly what *you* want. This is a sign that manifestation is close, though not yet guaranteed, because this situation is also a test of character from the universe. Can you be happy for that person, even though you are still waiting for it to happen? A classic example of this is if you are looking for love or trying to start a family, when a sibling or close friend suddenly announces they're getting married or having a baby. It can feel like a kick in the teeth, and trigger a lot of envy, but you should be gracious and congratulate them on their exciting news.

If you act on jealousy by being spiteful, sulky or competitive, it could derail your spells, because you have proven that you are not coming from a place of love, gratitude, and abundance, but from a place of envy, poverty, and ego.

Just because someone achieves something you want doesn't mean that you can no longer achieve it too. There is enough success for everyone, and the world is an abundant place. Their achievement hasn't taken anything away from you, but if a scarcity mind-set leads you to act enviously, you are only sabotaging your own success for the future. Instead, be grateful that your goal is so close! Take it as a sign that you are on the right track, that you are putting out the right spells and vibrations for manifestation to occur.

Being close to someone who gets what you want is not easy, but by being kind and gracious, you will prove to the universe that you, too, are ready for the success of your spells and the achievement of your goals. Be as happy for them as you would want them to be for you. Some goals are so common that there are bound to be others who get there first; try not to take it personally.

Keep in mind that jealousy will only prevent your own progress. It is a poison you feed to yourself, and it will do nothing to derail the success of those around you, so be happy for them and take it as a sign that your own success isn't far behind.

CAN SPELLS GO WRONG?

Sometimes a spell might not work very well, or it might not work in the way you thought it would. Often this is simply a case of rewording and tweaking the original spell. For magic to be effective, you need to be clear and specific as to what you are casting for. For example, if you cast a spell to bring a new companion into your life, you might find that you manifest a pet rather than a lover! If it is a lover you want, that is what your spell should focus on. Likewise, if all you want is a fling, make that clear in the spell or you might end up attracting someone who is looking to settle down. "Heartbreaker" is never a good nickname.

Being specific is the key to a successful spell. Don't leave it open to interpretation, because the universe doesn't understand nuance or vague suggestions. Be clear, be specific, and be bold. Magic will usually manifest *something*, so clarity is essential. It is rare that a spell has no effect whatsoever, because you are sending energy out into the universe, and that energy has to transform and come back to you in some way.

If you think your spell hasn't worked, check that all your correspondences etc. were in alignment with one another and with your goal. If they are, then you can always recast the spell. As mentioned earlier, some big goals need spells to be repeated over time to bring about manifestation. If the spells still don't seem to be working, it could be that what you are asking for isn't for your highest good.

If this is the case, another path will be offered to you, one that suits you much better. So don't lose heart. The universe really *is* on your side.

HOW TO MANAGE THE POWER OF MAGIC

Everyone holds a spark of magic inside them, a personal source of power that they can use to manifest their goals and ambitions. When you cast a spell, you are weaving together your personal power with the greater power of the universe. These two powers are what create magic and manifestation. This magical power is a form of energy, so it can never be diminished, it simply changes shape and form. You send energy out into the world when you cast a spell, and that energy changes form, returning to you as the manifestation of your goal. This is why your spells should be cast with a positive mind-set, to bring back positive results.

Some spells take more energy than others. A spell to manifest a new home would take significantly more power than a spell to find a parking place. That's why large goals require repeated spells: they need more energy. Likewise, several people working together in a coven can do more with one spell than a solitary practitioner can, again because there is more energy involved.

Managing energy is all part of being a witch or magical practitioner. As you cast a spell, you will feel the energy and excitement build until the spell is released. This could mean burning, burying, or scattering spell ingredients, to release the power of the magic. Building energy is an intrinsic aspect of spell-casting and it has its own guidelines, known as the Law of the Power, which is:

1. To Know
2. To Dare
3. To Will
4. To Be Silent

What this essentially means is that you must know what type of spell you are going to cast, and for what purpose. You must then have the courage to cast the spell and

will it into being. The final rule can be the hardest to follow for some people, because you must remain silent about what you have done.

Witches do not discuss the spells they cast until manifestation has occurred. Talking about the spell is thought to reduce the power and the possibility of it working. Have you ever told someone of an exciting new opportunity or romance, only to have the whole thing fall through? That's why it's important to remain silent about the spells you've cast. Don't diminish its power by gossiping about it. After all, it is no one else's business what you get up to with a candle!

TYPES OF MAGIC AND SPELLS

There are many kinds of magic, and different witches prefer different spells. Some like to work with candles, others prefer to use living plants. Hedge Witches work predominantly with herbs, Kitchen Witches with potions and food spells, Green Witches with the earth and the forest, and Scribe Witches with runes, sigils (magic symbols), and the written word. It must be said, however, that most witches work with most types of magic; we just have preferences for certain tools and spells. Here are some of the most popular types of spell.

PETITION SPELLS

Petition magic involves writing down your intention and releasing the spell by destroying the paper, either by burning it and scattering the ashes or ripping it up and disposing of it. Petition magic is the preferred spell of the Scribe Witch, who might also choose to incorporate runes and sigils. It is a very simple spell and requires only a pen and a sheet of paper. So it is perfect for quick spells that need to be cast in the moment. It requires little preparation and can be performed anywhere. It works by setting down your intention in ink on paper, then releasing it to the universe. That way you are petitioning the universe with a particular aim in mind, just as you might petition a politician to bring about certain policies. You can use this type of spell by itself or in conjunction with other kinds of magic, such as candle or poppet magic (see below). It is extremely effective and versatile.

POPPET SPELLS

Poppet magic is a type of sympathetic magic, which basically means that like attracts like, so whatever happens to the poppet should have an impact on the person it represents. We have all seen examples of poppet magic in horror films, where someone is sticking pins in a voodoo doll to cause harm. But in truth poppet magic is a gentle practice, often used in healing or love spells. To begin with, some kind of poppet—a doll or puppet—is fashioned by the witch. Poppets can be made from dough (like a gingerbread man), clay, yarn, string, a hankie, cardboard, or paper. One thing all poppet spells have in common, however, is the tag-lock—something that links it to the person it is meant to represent. This is usually hair from a hairbrush or comb, which is added to the doll's stuffing or fixed to its head. Once the doll has been tagged with the hair, it represents a real person and can be used in positive spells for healing. Obviously, this kind of spell can be misused, so it should only be used for positive spells that will benefit the person, and with their express permission.

CANDLE SPELLS

Candle magic is a staple in most magical spells and rituals, largely because the candle represents all four elements in one. The wax represents earth, the flame is fire, the melting wax is water, and the smoke is air. This means that candle magic is very powerful, and it is a core ingredient of most spells. Different-colored candles are used to represent different things. Large candles can be burned over a period of time to bring about a big goal, while a simple tea-light can be burned each day to maintain the light of love or abundance in your life. Candles are also a great base for other forms of magic. You can make candle spells as simple or as complex as you want. You can inscribe words, runes, or sigils into the wax to incorporate scribe magic, or anoint them with essential oils and roll them in dried herbs to incorporate hedge witchery. There is a lot of power in candle spells, and there are many for you to try. No witch worth her wand would ever run out of candles

and tea-lights, because they are so useful. In a pinch, magic can be made with a basic white candle and nothing else, so the box of candles you keep under the sink in case of a power outage could be all that you need.

CORD SPELLS

Cord spells are also called *witches' ladders*. They are a form of magic that uses a length of cord or ribbon in which knots are tied to manifest something or bind it to you. Traditionally, nine knots would be tied into the cord to form the witches' ladder, as an incantation is spoken as each knot is tied. Cords can also be used in banishing spells, to cut something from you, using a cord to represent that which no longer serves you. Cord rituals to manifest something are kept safe until manifestation has occurred,

when the knots are released and the cord is cleansed, ready to be used again. In banishing spells, the severed cord is usually buried in the ground, but in binding spells it is left permanently in place.

CONTAINMENT SPELLS

Containment spells are used to bring together a variety of spell ingredients to bring about a certain goal. Often, they use small jars or pouches filled with crystals, herbs, charms, and the written petition for the goal. These jars are kept in a special place, for example on the witch's altar, by the front door or hearth, or beside the bed, depending on what the purpose of the spell jar is. Pouches can be carried by the witch to manifest a specific outcome. Containment spells can also be used to negate any negative energy that is coming your way by placing a representation of that energy in a container, adding a binding agent such as glue or ice, and then hiding the container from sight.

VISUALIZATION SPELLS

While all spells require a certain amount of visualization in that you must be able to keep your goal in mind as you cast the spell, some rely on this skill more than others. Spells that help you connect with the elementals, or fey spirits, are one example. Power animal spells usually require strong

the process of writing a Book of Shadows or magical poetry. Basically, scribe magic is the art of writing your goal as if it has already happened, so you are in effect writing your future. It is a powerful and enjoyable technique, but it is also dependent on an aptitude for writing, so it is not for everyone.

NATURAL MAGIC

Natural magic, or folk magic, is a type of spell that uses elements of nature, such as seashells, pebbles, pine cones, acorns, crystals, leaves, flowers, snow, rainwater, and so on. Most spells incorporate some aspect of natural magic, and it is the linchpin of all witchcraft.

visualization techniques too. If you have difficulty with visualization, just think of it as magical daydreaming, for that is what it is. As long as you can hold an image in your mind as you cast the spell or make an invocation, there is no reason why your elemental and totem spells should not work.

As you can see from this (by no means exhaustive) list, there are many types of spells. In this book you will find examples of most of the spells mentioned here, often in combination with one another to build up the power. You can take aspects from here and there to build up a ritual, or use snippets to create unique spells. Magic is experimental, and what works for you might not work for someone else. That's because we each have natural abilities when it comes to magic, so while scribe magic works for me, you might prefer herb spells. Go with your instincts, and don't be afraid to try new things; that's the only way you'll discover where your own magical skills lie.

SCRIBE MAGIC

Scribe magic is the art of writing for manifestation. This kind of spell involves written affirmations and incantations, runes and magical alphabets, or drawing symbols to represent your goal. Keeping a magical journal is also a form of scribe magic because you are documenting your journey for future reference. Scribe magic can be anything from writing goals, affirmations, and petitions to dreaming up your ideal life on the page. It could be

CHAPTER THREE

POWER PLAY

Y~~ou~~ have the potential to blaze a path of magic through your life, using spell-craft to influence your choices, decisions, and dilemmas. You can use the craft of magic to attract the right kind of people to you and open doors to the right places and opportunities. Before you do any of this, however, you need to understand your obligations as a practitioner of magic.

Like any other kind of power and authority, magic comes with the weight of responsibility. It will give you autonomy over your life, but you must ensure that your magic doesn't interfere with the lives of others. There are guidelines you should follow to get the most from your spells while also safeguarding the free will of others.

ETHICS OF MAGIC

Before you cast any kind of ritual or spell, you should ask yourself if it will have an impact on anyone other than yourself. Witches do not cast spells on other people, but we do weave a web of magic around ourselves in order to attract the things we want. What does this mean in practice? Well, it means that you should never cast spells for another person without their permission. This includes magic for healing the sick and helping someone who is dealing with addiction. It can be difficult watching someone you care about struggle, but unless you have permission to cast spells for them,

try to help in more mundane ways instead.

There is a good reason for this, and it is all about free will. In casting spells without permission you are effectively tampering with someone's free will. You could also be preventing them from learning a spiritual or life lesson with your interference. By all means, talk to them to see how they feel about magic. But unless you have permission to work spells on their behalf, stick to casting only for yourself. While this might seem selfish, it is really the kindest and most ethical option. If someone you love is sick, but you know they wouldn't like the idea of magic, then instead of casting healing spells for them, cast spells for strength and service around yourself, so you can be there when they need you, and so you are more inspired to help in a way *they* find comforting.

Another example would be that of love spells. You should only cast spells on yourself in order to attract more love into your life. Love cannot be forced, even by magic. It is a gift that must be offered freely, without conditions attached. So if you want more romance in your life, cast a spell to attract more romantic situations toward you, rather than one to turn your partner into Casanova! Keep in mind the ripple effect of any spells you cast and try to ensure that they do not encroach on the free will of anyone else.

THE THREEFOLD LAW

One of the reasons witches are such sticklers for protecting free will is because of the Threefold Law, which states that whatever you send out magically will come back to you with three times the force and three times the consequences. This is why you should never cast in the spirit of envy, vengeance, or spite, because essentially, you are only hurting yourself in the long run, when all those emotions are directed back at you in some way.

The Threefold Law means that whatever you send out will come back to you, so if you are sending out positive, happy vibrations, you will receive positive and happy opportunities in return. Likewise, if you are sending out negative, complaining vibes then you are attracting more negative

things to complain about. In short, do good deeds and good things will come to you. Do bad deeds and…well, I wouldn't want to be in your shoes when they return!

In Wiccan belief, we often refer to the Threefold Law as the Harm None rule, which simply states: "*Harm none, do what you will.*" This little mantra reminds us to make sure we keep our thoughts, words, deeds, and magic positive in nature, so that we are not inadvertently encroaching on someone's free will or causing harm to another living creature. It is a life-enhancing law to live by, for it means that we are always mindful of how our actions might impact other people, animals, and the natural world.

EMOTIONS

Your emotions are the fuel to your spells. How you are feeling when you cast a spell can have an impact on how well it works. Likewise, so can your state of health. Generally speaking, the more positive and upbeat you are when you cast a spell, the better it will work. But what about those occasions when you can't be upbeat, but you need a little magic on your side?

Say you have suffered a bereavement, or you have the flu—what then? At times such as these, it is best to work only gentle spells rather than full rituals. Simple acts of petition, crystal, or candle magic can give

home, or a spell for justice so the police could catch the burglars. That way, you turn a negative event into positive spell-craft. Just because an *emotion* is considered negative doesn't mean that the *magic* you make with it will be. You can turn a negative emotion into a positive outcome by channeling it as fuel and directing it toward a positive goal. Just keep the Harm None rule at the forefront of your mind as you release these emotions into your magic.

SET YOUR INTENTION

We talked about intentions a little earlier. If emotion is the *fuel* for your magic, then intention is the *vehicle* in which it travels. You need both to cast an effective spell; otherwise, like a car without gas or gas without a car, the magic is going nowhere. Where many neophyte witches fail, however, is to assume that you state your intention once and the job is done. It isn't quite that simple.

you the boost you need without taking too much of your energy; remember, effective magic requires your energy to work. Try not to cast big spells if you are sick, because you need your energy to recover. Instead, light a candle or hold a crystal and ask for healing energies to surround you.

All emotions can be fuel for magic, as long as they are directed in the right way. While some witches believe you should not cast in anger, others claim that it is vibrant energy that should be directed to your goal, as long as you adhere to the Harm None rule. Imagine that you were burglarized. Understandably, you'd be angry about such a violation of your space and privacy, but instead of directing this anger toward the perpetrators of the crime in a spell for vengeance, you could channel it into a powerful protection spell around your

Intention is all about mindset, belief, and behavior. You can state the intention that you will find love, but unless you also *believe* that you are lovable and *act* from a loving heart, the intention falls flat. This is because your actions and behaviors are not in alignment with your magical goal. In short, you are not backing up your spell with complementary actions that support your intention.

To set a true intention, you must first of all believe that it is possible for you to have what you are casting for. You must know deep in your heart that you are worthy of it and that you deserve to have it. You must act as if it is already coming to you and feel a sense of certainty that you will have it. Finally, you must make yourself ready to receive it by making space for it in your life. This process is the same regardless of the goal.

If setting an intention were as simple as just writing it down on a piece of paper, then we would all be manifesting our heart's desires all the time! Writing down your intentions does help, especially if you can see it every day. This will help keep you on track with regards to your mind-set, but it is really just a visual cue to set the intention internally, within your heart, mind, and soul. Only when you have achieved this, when you are living and breathing your intention on a daily basis, will manifestation of your spell occur, because you are giving the universe a full picture of what you want it to reflect back at you.

For magic to be effective, your intention must be clear and strong. Self-doubt can slow down your spells or stop them from working altogether. If you can't imagine yourself juggling the responsibilities of self-employment, then your spells to become a full-time business owner are likely to fall flat, especially if you've never even set up shop, as it were. It is essential that you take steps to live in alignment with your magical goal even before it has manifested. This is how you teach yourself to believe it's possible.

Setting an intention is not just a case of daydreaming or wishful thinking. It is the act of committing to a specific goal, of knowing what your motivations are and how you need to change your behavior in order to accomplish it. It's about living proactively and moving closer to your goal on a daily basis, or at least keeping it at the forefront of your mind. It's about knowing why you want something and what you hope to gain from having it. It's about mentally and emotionally stepping into your future, even before that future exists in reality. Most importantly, it is a shift in

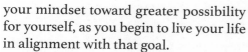

your mindset toward greater possibility for yourself, as you begin to live your life in alignment with that goal.

It is your intention that helps support the magical process, and you can't cast effective spells without it. Think carefully about how you word your intention for each spell you cast, and what you need to do to back it up in your day-to-day actions.

As you can see, setting your intentions is a ritual in its own right, and it can be quite time-consuming until you get used to it. Once your spells start to work and you realize that you can co-create your reality with the help of the universe and a little magic, it will become second nature. To put it in the simplest of terms:

Emotion + Intention
= Magical Manifestation

TIMING

When you perform your magic will have an effect on how well it works. While emergency spells can and should be cast if a crisis occurs, when spells are planned, you will want to ensure that you are casting them at the right time. All the spells in this book clearly state when they should be cast, but once you begin to create your own spells and rituals, you will need to have a working knowledge of magical timing and how it works.

THE LUNAR CYCLE

Magic is created in accordance with the phases of the moon. This is the most important aspect of magical timing, because the magnetic pull of the moon works with the universal tides to either pull something toward you or take it away. That being the case, your spells to manifest something should be cast during the period from new to full moon, whereas spells that banish something should be cast from full to waning moon. Below is a brief overview of how the different phases of the moon can be used in your magic.

New Moon

This is the beginning of the lunar cycle, although the moon cannot actually be seen in the sky until a few days after the

new moon. For this reason, the start of the new moon phase is sometimes known as dark moon, and is typically a time of rest. As soon as the first sliver of light appears—a delicate crescent moon that looks like a backwards C—it is time to start thinking about what you want the next lunar cycle to bring you. The new moon is a time for sowing seeds of new projects, weighing the pros and cons of a situation, assessing the need for a change in your patterns, and so forth. Remember that all seeds are sown in darkness, to grow with the light. Now is the time to decide what you want.

Waxing Crescent

The light increases as the crescent moon fills leftward. This is the time when you set your intention—set your mind on exactly what you want. You don't need to know how you will achieve the goal, just set your intention and allow the universe to figure out the details.

First Quarter Moon

In this phase, the moon looks as if it has been cut in half—half of it is illuminated by the sun, the other half remains in darkness. Now is the time to take action on your intentions, so update your resumé or start applying for jobs if a career change is your goal. Make a positive start on a new project. Get out more and meet new people if you want to draw friends to you. Make a start on your goal, even if only in a small way.

Waxing Gibbous

The moon now appears to be three quarters full, with most of it brightening our night sky. Now is the time to start walking your talk. It's not enough to have a goal; you need to take consistent action and work toward it. It is a collaboration, and you need to put in the effort too. At this time, the energies are growing stronger and magnetically pulling in your intention, so help it along with positive action.

Full Moon

The full moon lights up the night sky, and her effect can be felt all over the world.

This is a time of abundance, of goals coming to fruition and laboring on long-term ambitions. The full moon offers a boost of energy if you are flagging on your aspirations, lending much-needed energy to your goal. The energy of the full moon can be felt for three nights in a row—the night before, the night of, and the night after. This is also the most powerful time for all kinds of magic, divination, and spell-casting, so don't waste it!

Waning Gibbous

As the moon begins to wane, it is time to show gratitude for what this lunar cycle has brought you. Reflect on what worked and what projects are still in progress. Big ambitions take more than one lunar cycle to manifest, so use this time to assess where you are on the path to achievement and reflect on what your next steps should be. Think about what worked and what you would like to do better in the next lunar cycle.

Last/Third Quarter Moon

This is the time to start releasing anything that no longer serves you. Let go of old grudges, bad relationships, mistakes, toxic habits and so on. In this phase, the moon requires you to be honest with yourself, to identify the toxic behaviors and bad habits that might be contributing to a negative situation so you can release those, too.

Waning Crescent/Balsamic Moon

This phase marks the end of the lunar cycle, when the moon shows up in our skies as the classic fairy-tale crescent. It is a time to reflect and move deeper into self-awareness. This is a good time to cast banishing spells as the moon's energy helps pull things away from you (the word "balsamic" refers to its restorative nature). Slowly the light will fade, night by night, until we are back at the dark moon and the cycle begins once more, so it is never too late for a fresh start. Each moon cycle offers a new opportunity to begin again.

DAYS OF THE WEEK

Each day of the week is associated with a planet, and therefore has its own energies that you can tap into magically. Although you don't have to wait for a given day to perform a spell, casting on a particular day can give your spells an added boost of power, so if you *can* cast on the right day, do so.

Sunday

Ruled by the Sun, this is a golden day to cast for success, abundance, growth, happiness, joy, and greater achievement or acknowledgment of your accomplishments. Sunday is the day to cast spells designed to get you noticed for all the right reasons.

Monday

Ruled by the Moon, this is the day for spells of intuition, dreams, ambition, psychic ability, protecting innocents, and setting goals. It is a good day to cast glamour spells or enchantments, and to create an air of mystery around yourself.

Tuesday

Ruled by Mars, the Roman god of war, this is the day to work toward conflict resolution, self-defense, protection, and boundary setting. Mars's energy can help you speak your mind and stand up for yourself and others, but use it cautiously or it could lead to aggressive behavior. Aim for peace, rather than victory at any cost.

Wednesday

Ruled by Mercury, the Roman god of communication, this is the day to cast spells of communication, partnerships, collaborations, creativity, arts and crafts, reunions, and reconciliations. This is the best day to send off resumés, apply for jobs, or set up interviews and business meetings. If you need help with confidence in your communications, make Mercury your friend.

Thursday

Ruled by the mighty Jupiter and associated with the Norse god Thor, Thursday is a great day to cast for all aspects of financial control, career and business growth, wealth building, decision making, and stability. With Thor on your side, you can also work magic to protect your interests and defend against saboteurs who might be trying to move against you—for example, to prevent being outbid in a real-estate deal. This is a day for practicalities, but also for standing strong, staking and maintaining your claim.

Friday

Ruled by Venus and associated with the Norse goddess Freya, Friday is the day for matters of the heart, be they romantic or

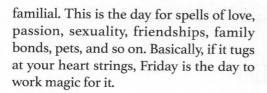

familial. This is the day for spells of love, passion, sexuality, friendships, family bonds, pets, and so on. Basically, if it tugs at your heart strings, Friday is the day to work magic for it.

Saturday

Ruled by Saturn, Saturday is the day of banishment and sometimes melancholy. This is the day to cast spells to remove things from your life that no longer serve you, or to come to terms with feelings of depression and low mood. Saturn is also associated with the Roman winter feast of Saturnalia, which was held between December 17th and 23rd, and is the origin of a good Saturday night out, so this is the best day to cast for fun, frolic, and adventure.

HOW LONG WILL IT TAKE?

If you are new to magic, you might be wondering how long it will take for your spells to work and manifestation to occur. That depends on what you are casting for. In general, larger goals and spells take longer to work than smaller ones, and repeat casting is usually needed, but that doesn't mean they're not working. Often there will be signs that your magic is in play, as we mentioned earlier, so be on the lookout for these, and don't lose heart. If you just want some indication that you have the ability to cast an effective spell, then cast

for something small and simple, such as a parking space or a free cup of coffee, and see how long that takes to manifest in your life. Such small spells usually work in a day or two and offer the reassurance you need that your magic is effective.

Medium goals, say for attracting new friends or opportunities, can take a full lunar cycle before you begin to see signs that they are working, while big life goals, such as starting a family, moving to a new location, or changing careers will take several months before they start to manifest. Just keep the faith and repeat the spells for larger goals. If it is something that is meant for you, it will always find its way to you; if it's not, then trust that something even better will come along instead.

CHAPTER FOUR

SPELLBOUND!

Casting a spell is similar to conducting a science experiment. You gather the equipment required, use your knowledge and instincts to guide you, and make a note of what worked and what didn't. Then you repeat the process until you get the results you want or learn something new. Like any other experiment, magic involves preparations, and has its own tool kit.

No two practitioners will experience exactly the same results, even if they are casting the same spell. This is because magic utilizes your unique energy, so the way it manifests will be as unique as you are. Your magic will work in the way that is best for you.

ELEMENTS OF MAGIC

Most spells combine your power with that of nature and the universe, using the four elements of earth, air, fire and water. These elements make up the whole of the natural world, so adding them into spell-craft is a powerful approach and one that witches have used for centuries. If you look at any spell book, you will see these four elements pop up time and again. That's because our survival depends on them, and each is essential to us. Each element also represents a particular kind of magic. In general, a spell will incorporate at least one of these elements in some form.

Earth

Earth power is green and growing, changing and renewing. It is alive with potential. In magic, earth power is represented by herbs, plants, leaves, cones, crystals, and so on. Earth spells tend to focus on growth, abundance, expansion, transformation, and grounding.

Air

Like the wind, the power of air can be soft and gentle or strong and raging. Its power is changeable and is represented by burning incense, smudge bundles, feathers, fans, and images of birds or clouds. Air spells tend to be cast for inspiration, creativity, communication, ambition, momentum, and the arts. Music is associated with the powers of air, especially wind instruments.

dreams, intuition, psychic ability, cleansing, and purifying.

TOOLS OF MAGIC

Although spells can be performed successfully with few tools, there are several items that most witches keep handy. Most can be found around the house and adapted to magical use, so there's no need to spend a lot of money.

Athame

This is a magical knife. It is used to direct energy, or to carve sigils and words into spell candles. Traditionally, it should have a black handle, and the blade should be dulled to render it harmless. You can use any knife that you find appealing, however, from a basic kitchen knife to a fancy letter opener. The athame is attuned with the element of fire.

Wand

A wand can be used as an alternative to the athame, for directing energy. It can be made of crystal or wood, and is attuned with the element of air.

Pentacle

This is a round disc decorated with a pentagram or five-pointed star. It is probably the most useful tool of spell-craft, as witches place candles, crystals, and so on on the

Fire

A balance must be struck when using fire in spells, because it has the power to destroy everything in its path. In general, fire magic is contained in a heat-proof vessel to keep it from getting out of hand. Fire spells are cast for passion, love, and desire, and fire magic is used in banishing spells too.

Water

Like air, water can be gentle or destructive. This element can be temperamental to say the least! In magic, water is represented by a chalice of water or wine, seashells, pebbles, and images of fish and marine life. Driftwood and seaweed can also be used, combining the elements of water and earth. Water spells are usually cast for matters of emotional balance, healing, pentacle to charge them with magical energy. It is attuned with the element of earth. You can make one by drawing a five-pointed star on a plate or disc.

Chalice

Your chalice can be any stemmed drinking vessel. A simple wine glass will suffice. The chalice is attuned with the element of water and is used to hold ritual wine.

Broom/Besom

A traditional broom is used in cleansing rituals to sweep away negative energy. They can be decorated with ribbons, feathers, and carvings down the stave.

Cauldron

An iron cauldron or fire-proof pan is used to contain fire. This means that you can safely burn fire spells in it, or place a candle in it as part of a ritual celebration. It can also be used as a divination tool. Like the chalice, it represents the element of water.

Cloak and Crown

These are by no means essential, and are reminiscent of high ceremonial magic, such as Wicca. But some practitioners like to wear a special robe, gown, or cloak when they are in a ritual setting. Crowns were used to denote hierarchy in a coven, but a simple flower or moon crown can be worn

to help the practitioner step into a magical frame of mind. Cloaks can be useful when conducting spells and rituals outdoors, especially on cold evenings. It must be stressed, however, that this is a matter of personal preference, and is not a necessary tool of magic.

Consumables

Most of the spells in this book use herbs, candles, oils, crystals, ribbons, and so on. If you are on a budget, this is where you should focus your spending, as all the other tools can be found around the home and adapted to magical use.

CREATING A MAGICAL ALTAR

Once you have gathered your tools, you are ready to create an altar in your home and dedicate it to your practice. It can be any

shelf, windowsill, or desk. Traditionally, the altar should be placed in the north or east of a room. Altars always represent the four elements, plus divinity, and there are certain items that should be placed on it.

You should stand two white candles on either side, toward the back of the altar. These represent the element of fire.

Between the two candles, place something that represents divinity: a statue or picture of a goddess or a god, or both. Or it could be something more abstract, such as a crystal or a plant.

An incense holder is useful, as you can use it to represent air, and also to burn incense as an offering of gratitude, even when you don't plan on casting a full ritual. Place it to the east or right side of the altar.

Water is usually represented by a chalice or any stemmed drinking vessel, placed at the west or left side of the altar. As an alternative, you can use a seashell or pebble.

Finally, you should add something to represent the element of earth. This could be a plant, crystal, flowers, or your pentacle, which belongs front and center.

Other items you might like to use include crystals, seashells, feathers, pine cones, or a jar of salt for purification. Make it as magical and beautiful as you can, and place your Book of Spells close by. Be aware that your altar will evolve, growing as you grow into your magic.

SYMBOLS OF MAGIC

Certain symbols and sigils are seen time and again, each with its own meaning. Below is a list of the most common symbols used in magical practice, though this is by no means exhaustive. Feel free to experiment.

Pentagram

This is the magical five-pointed star, not to be confused with the Star of David, which has six points. The pentagram is the most common symbol used in magic. It is carved upon the pentacle disc, into candles, written on spell papers, and so on. It represents the forces of positive magic, with each point of the star associated with one of the elements. The top point represents the energy of the universe, or the light of spirit and divinity.

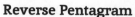

Reverse Pentagram

The reverse pentagram has a bad reputation; non-magical people tend to associate it with negative magic. In Wiccan circles, however, the reverse pentagram—two points upward and one point facing downward—has nothing to do with negative magic or evil influences. The shape suggests the horns and beard of the Horned God of Wicca, so it is used to attune with the male aspect of nature and divinity. There is nothing sinister about this symbol, and it can be used in positive magic or in meditation to reflect on the reverse energies of nature, such as darkness, decay, and winter. But use the reverse pentagram carefully, as it can make people a little nervous.

The Triple Goddess

The sigil of the Triple Goddess is used to connect spells with the divine feminine and with the triple aspects of womanhood: Maiden, Mother and Crone. It is another symbol that frequently comes up in spells and rituals.

The Triquetra

This is another symbol of trinity and the divine female, yet it can also be used to represent the past, present, and future, symbolizing the interwoven thread that links all three.

Ankh

This Egyptian symbol is often seen in magical circles. It has become a popular sigil, used to represent immortality, reincarnation, the afterlife, and the sacred journey of the undying, eternal spirit.

Eye of Horus

Another Egyptian symbol, this is associated with wisdom, clarity, the spiritual vision of the third eye, psychic ability, and the realms of the unseen. It is often used as a protection device to guard against harm both seen and unseen.

Equal-Armed Cross

This sigil symbolizes the meeting of the four directions, the four winds, and the four elements. It is also used to represent the four seasonal thresholds of Spring Equinox, Midsummer, Autumnal Equinox and Midwinter. It is used in magic for grounding and stability. It is associated with polarity and duality.

Celtic Cross

The Celtic Cross embodies all the symbolism of the Equal-Armed Cross, but also has the protective powers of the sacred circle, making it a very powerful symbol.

MAGICAL CORRESPONDENCES

Any tool that is used in spell-craft is called a correspondence. There are correspondences for all different types of magic, and you will need to know what these are when you start writing your own spells. Below is a list of Magical Correspondences for the most popular types of magic, so that if you do not have what a spell calls for, you can look at the Correspondences and switch to something else that has the same associations. This should work just as well, and it will stand you in good stead when it's time to write your own spells. Of course, if you have had great success with a particular herb or crystal, keep using it, but in general, these are the Correspondences that work well for these types of magic.

Magical Correspondences for Love

Colors: red, pink, lilac, white
Crystals: carnelian, rose quartz, ruby, diamond, clear quartz, citrine
Herbs: rose, rosemary, peony, lavender, lilac, elderflower, myrtle, ivy
Oils: rose, geranium, ylang ylang, lavender, neroli
Incense: rose, strawberry, ylang ylang, night queen, sandalwood

Magical Correspondences for Prosperity

Colors: green, gold, silver, white
Crystals: aventurine, jade, iron pyrite, clear quartz
Herbs: basil, bay, cinnamon, tea leaves, sage, mint, sunflower
Oils: patchouli, frankincense, sunflower, rape seed
Incense: cinnamon, frankincense, night queen, patchouli, dragon's blood

Magical Correspondences for Protection

Colors: black, gray, dark blue, purple, dark red, white
Crystals: hematite, onyx, amethyst, sodalite, smoky quartz
Herbs: thistle, rosemary, basil, holly, turmeric, garlic, mugwort, foxglove
Oils: tea tree, bergamot, eucalyptus, cedar wood, pine

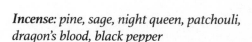

Incense: pine, sage, night queen, patchouli, dragon's blood, black pepper

Magical Correspondences for Power
Colors: black, purple, red, white
Crystals: hematite, amethyst, clear quartz, smoky quartz, snowy quartz
Herbs: lavender, rosemary, basil, sage, mugwort
Oils: tea tree, patchouli, eucalyptus, pine
Incense: pine, sage, night queen, patchouli, dragon's blood

CREATING A SACRED SPACE

Most practitioners cast their spells in a space that has been ritually constructed and cleansed. It doesn't need to be a large space; a small area of a room or a quiet, sheltered spot outdoors would be adequate. The space should give you access to the altar, or enable you to set up an altar on the ground. To begin, smudge the area by wafting an incense stick or smudge bundle around the entire sacred space. This acts as a ritual cleansing.

All magic is performed inside the space. The circle of magic is a realm between the worlds, which means that it hangs in the ether, deep in the womb of sacred creativity, creating a portal that allows the magic of transformation to be birthed. The circle is where magic begins and the seeds of manifestation are sown. It is often referred to as being *between the worlds*, meaning that it is of both the magical and mundane realms of existence. Some practitioners refer to the circle as being on the *Astral Plane*, which again refers to the fact that it is in neither this world nor the next, but somewhere in between.

The purpose of the circle is to contain the energy you raise as you work magic, so it doesn't leak away from the spell. That way, the energy is only released when the practitioner directs it to be so. The circle also acts as a boundary of protection around you as you work. A magic circle can be cast as a protective device around your home, your car, or yourself, too, so it is a handy skill.

Casting a Circle

To cast a circle, you will need your athame, wand, or finger. Stand in front of your altar and walk, or turn if the space is small, in a circle with your wand (or whatever) held out. Move three times clockwise, visualizing a blue or white light coming from your athame, wand, or finger and creating a circle all around you and your altar. As you do so, say:

I conjure this circle of sacred power
Protect my magic this witching hour
In the great void of darkness,
   I conjure this shield
In my magical fortress, this circle is sealed

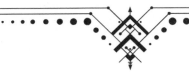

Calling the Quarters

Each quarter of the circle is governed by one of the elements. These elements should also be called, or invoked, before any magic is performed. Since spell-craft is all about attuning with nature, we invoke the four elements that make up our world—earth, air, fire and water. To begin the invocations, go to the north of your circle, raise your arms high in invocation and say:

> *Elemental guardians of the north*
> *Powers of abundance and growth*
> *I invoke your presence and ask you to*
>   *protect this sacred space*

Move to the east of the circle and repeat the process, saying:

> *Elemental guardians of the east*
> *Powers of creativity and communication*
> *I invoke your presence and ask you to*
>   *protect this sacred space*

Move to the south of your circle say:

> *Elemental guardians of the south*
> *Powers of love and passion*
> *I invoke your presence and ask you to*
>   *protect this sacred space*

Finally, go to the west of the circle and invoke the final quarter, saying:

> *Elemental guardians of the west*
> *Powers of intuition and emotion*
> *I invoke your presence and ask you to*
>   *protect this sacred space*

Move to the middle of the circle and say:

> *Welcome, spirits and guardians four*
> *To this world between worlds of*
>   *magical lore*

You are now ready to work rituals with your chosen deities, cast the spells of your choice, or perform divinations. Once you have completed your magical tasks, you will need to release the guardians you have invoked. Do this by going in reverse order, starting in the west, and saying to each quarter:

> *The spell is cast, the magic is bright*
> *Guardians I release you*
> *In peace, love, and light*

To Take Down the Circle

Once the magic is complete and the elemental guardians have been released, you need to take down the magic circle you have created. This is an indication that your spell has been released into the world so it can begin to manifest. Taking down the circle is easy. Simply walk three times around your sacred space in a counterclockwise direction, imagining

the light of the circle fading out as you say:

*The wise words of spell-craft have
now been spoken
This circle is open, but never broken*

EMERGENCY SPELLS

There might be occasions when you don't
have time to gather lots of tools, cast a full
circle or call in the quarters. In an emergency,
magic can still be made effectively with few
tools and little ceremony. If, for example,
you are at a hospital, you can cast a healing
spell using a cup of water by focusing your
intention on the water and visualizing the
healing benefits of that element, then
drinking the water to activate the spell.

However, most emergency spells are
cast in the home. Tea-lights are the best
tool for the job. Like all candles, they
represent the four elements in a single
tool. Hold one between your palms and
focus on the intention and the outcome
you are trying to manifest. This could be
a home repair, or simply a better day at
work. Once you can see the goal in your
mind, light the tea-light and allow it to
work its magic for you. State that you are
casting an emergency spell as you light
the flame, saying:

*In a fix I find myself, in dire straits of
woe*

*I resolve the issue with this spell and
let the magic go*

Emergency spells are usually quick to
resolve an issue, but don't be afraid to cast
them daily until a resolution is achieved. In
a pinch, or on the go, you can also use the
flame of a lighter. Have faith that you have
set magic in motion and that circumstances
will improve.

SILENT SPELLS

While most spells incorporate incantations
designed to be spoken out loud, not
everyone is comfortable with chanting.
So I have included some spells that do not
involve speaking. It should also be said that
any of the spells in this book can be turned
into silent spells simply by omitting the
incantations. It is nice, however, to have
some magic that is designed specifically
to be worked in silence.

Many spiritual disciplines use silence as
a form of worship and communion. It can
help deepen your understanding of yourself
and the natural world. It can open up the
channels of communication between you
and your spirit guides.

Maintaining silence isn't always easy, so
the silent spells are deliberately short and
sweet. Take note of anything you are drawn
to do during these spells, any inspiration
that comes to you amid the silence.

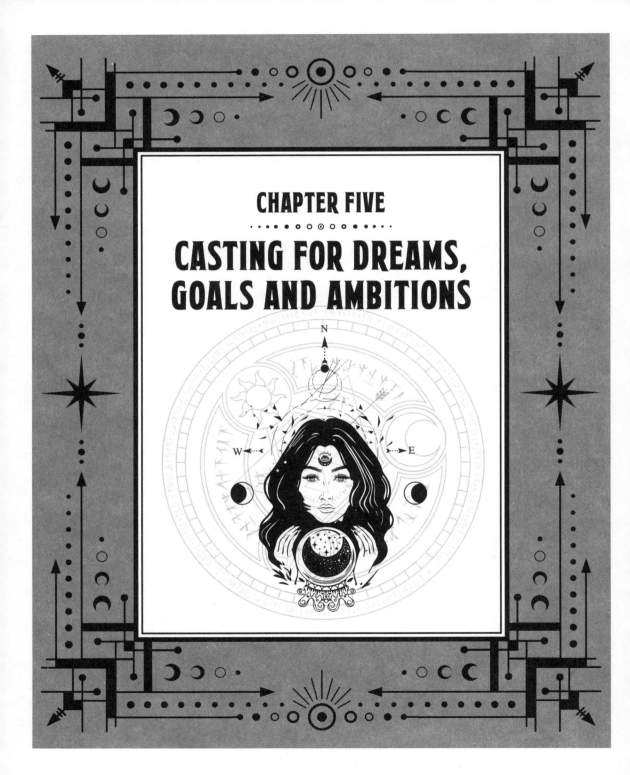

CHAPTER FIVE

. . . . . . ◦ ⊙ ◦ . . . . . .

CASTING FOR DREAMS, GOALS AND AMBITIONS

Having dreams and ambitions is an important aspect of keeping your life moving forward. Without a goal to aim for, life can become monotonous, routine and stagnant. As humans, we require a sense of growth and expansion to be happy and fulfilled. While downtime is needed to recharge, too much of it can be detrimental to your long-term success. As with anything else, striking a balance is the key.

Goal setting is an intrinsic part of spell-craft, but it should also be considered an intrinsic part of life. Without a clear direction, you will be buffeted around by the whims of others, and you might find yourself growing resentful when those around you achieve their dreams but you don't seem to be getting anywhere. This chapter will help you to determine what it is that you want from life and offer magical steps toward achieving it.

AMBITION IS A GOOD THING

Some people are naturally ambitious. For other people, ambition has to be developed and worked up like a muscle. They might believe that dreams are a waste of time because good things never happen to them, or that people who are successful have just been very lucky. While luck does play a part in any success story, there is a science behind ambition that shows that those who set a goal are more likely to be successful

than those who don't. It is also true that one success tends to lead to the next, leading to a snowball effect of achievement.

Ambition is good for your mental health, as long it is realistic. Not everyone can become a rock star or a famous actor, but most people can use their talents and interests to enhance their lives. Some ambitions have nothing to do with money and are more about a sense of achievement. Athletic ambitions, such as running a marathon or climbing a mountain, would fall into this category. You can have ambitions for your career, relationships, fitness, health, self-image, creativity and many other things.

Ambition is also good for your self-esteem, because it often leads to achievement. Achievement gives your confidence a boost and proves that you

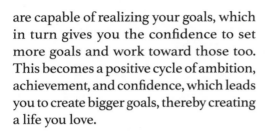

are capable of realizing your goals, which in turn gives you the confidence to set more goals and work toward those too. This becomes a positive cycle of ambition, achievement, and confidence, which leads you to create bigger goals, thereby creating a life you love.

Spell to Light the Spark of Ambition

Items required: a gold or silver candle and suitable holder, your athame or carving tool, sunflower oil, a little saffron (optional)
Timing: cast at noon, during the time of the full moon for greatest power of sun and moon energy

Take the items to your altar and think about what it means to be ambitious. How would you feel if you believed that you could achieve anything? What would your life look like? Imagine how much confidence you would have. Try to dream up these feelings as you hold the candle in your hands.

Visualize yourself living out your dreams and achieving your goals. When you are ready, carve the word *Ambition* into the length of the candle, then anoint it by rubbing the sunflower oil all over it, imbuing the candle with the sun's energies. If you are using saffron, sprinkle a small amount onto a paper towel and roll the anointed candle through the saffron so that it sticks to the oil, pulling the candle

toward you as you do so. Place the candle into the holder and light the wick as you chant these words nine times:

Ambition burns bright in me
The light of success shines down
   upon me
The sunlight empowers me
The moonlight guides me
Opportunity finds me
Achievement delights me
By earth, moon and sun
This magic is done

Leave the candle in place to burn down naturally, which can take several hours, so make sure you cast this spell when you will be at home to watch over the flame.

WHAT DO YOU REALLY WANT?

Half the fun of having ambition lies in deciding exactly what you want. This is where you get to dream of possibilities and see which one calls to you.

Spending time visualizing is part of the creative, magical process. Decide what you want and work toward that goal. A smaller goal is usually achieved more easily, so start with something simple to increase your confidence, then work up to bigger goals. Once you have a clear idea of your main ambitions and goals, use that idea to create a vision board.

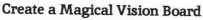

Create a Magical Vision Board

Items required: a large piece of poster board, images that represent your ambitions, a glue stick, patchouli oil, a pen
Timing: create your board at the time of the new moon, to bring all good things toward you

Making a vision board is a traditional way to set your intention and have your goals in front of you on a daily basis. While you can make digital versions on a computer, you will need to anoint your board with oil, so the old-fashioned poster-board variety is necessary for this spell. Find images that represent the things you are working toward—be it pictures of people working, traveling, enjoying a romantic dinner, getting married, and so on. Gather a collection of images, so that all the main aspects of your life are represented. Alternatively, create a vision board that focuses on a single goal.

Using the pen, draw a pentagram on the back of the board. This will help protect your dreams from negative energies and toxic influences. Take the patchouli oil and dab a little onto the four corners of the vision board. Next, glue all the images in place on the board and put it where you will see it every day. As you achieve the goals on the board, use a red, silver or gold pen to tick them off. This will give you a boost, as you see that you are moving closer to your dreams. Once you have checked off all the images, make a new board for your new goals.

Seven-Step Spell for Goal Manifestation

Items required: seven slips of paper, a tea-light holder you love, tea-lights, a pen
Timing: at the time of the full moon

This is an ongoing spell that takes time to complete, so you need to include it in your day-to-day routine. It works best for bigger goals, such as changing careers, moving, starting a family, and so on. Gather the items needed and begin by visualizing the goal as if you were already living it. Enjoy this part of the process and indulge in a little daydreaming. What does your

goal feel like to you? Once you can see the goal clearly, break it down into seven manageable steps. The first could be doing research, such as looking at real-estate ads, followed by seeing a mortgage broker, viewing a house and so on. Once you have seven clear steps, write one step on each of the slips of paper. Take the first piece of paper and read the first step out loud. This is an instruction to yourself, a command to make the first move and get the ball rolling.

Light a tea-light in the holder each evening and place all the spell papers close by. Each day, follow the command of the relevant step until you have achieved that aspect of the goal, then burn it in the flame of the tea-light. In burning the spell paper, you are indicating that you cannot go backward, but can only move toward your goal.

LUCK

There is more to a successful ambition than just hard work and goal setting. Luck and good fortune will also play a part, putting you in the right place at the right time. Here are a few mundane tips that you can use to start turning luck in your favor:

- **Be nice to the gatekeepers.** In all your dealings with your chosen industry or ambition, be nice to receptionists, personal assistants, secretaries, and so on. They are the gatekeepers to the world you wish to join, and they can make sure your correspondence reaches the right people. So be nice.

- **Use a charm offensive.** Aim to be pleasant and personable in all your interactions, and your name is more likely to be remembered for all the right reasons when new opportunities are up for grabs.

- **Don't just offer your services.** You need to offer something concrete, rather than just the gift of your services. Offer a business plan, a submission, a proposal, a demonstration—something that proves that you've put some thought into how you can be an asset.

Think of all this as laying the groundwork. You never know who you might meet, and it only takes one person to like you for doors to start swinging wide open.

Hard work will only get you so far. Luck alone can bring a fleeting success that burns bright in the moment, but soon burns out. However, hard work and good fortune working in tandem is how lasting success is brought to pass. Give Lady Luck a warm welcome by casting the following spell.

A Spell for Good Fortune

Items required: an ace of diamonds playing card, frankincense oil, a pen
Timing: during a waxing moon

Playing cards have long been used in spell-casting, so it is always a good idea to have an extra pack around the house that you can use solely for this purpose. This spell calls for the ace of diamonds. Take the card and write your full name and date of birth on the front. Dab it with a touch of frankincense oil on all four corners. Put the playing card face up on your pentacle, and place your hands palms up to receive, on either side of the pentacle.

Sit for a time and imagine lots of luck coming to you. Visualize meeting the right people, receiving invitations, having the right opportunities extended to you.

Imagine winning streaks, lucky breaks, windfalls, and blessings, all coming to you now. When you feel ready, chant the following words three times:

Lady Luck shines bright on me
All my dreams come true
In love and light there comes to me
Diamonds forged anew
Fate will open doors for me
This charm now paves the way
Opportunities now come to me
My luck is strong by night and day

CHAPTER SIX
CASTING FOR ABUNDANCE

Money is an issue for many people. Too much of it can be overwhelming, while too little can lead to destitution. Very few people are entirely comfortable with the amount of money they have; most people have some degree of money stress to contend with. While money should never be thought of as the root of all evil, it can be troublesome at times. In this chapter we will explore how you can use magic to become more abundant and prosperous, so that your money worries are few and fleeting.

WHAT IS ABUNDANCE?

Abundance is a state of plenty. It is about knowing you have enough for yourself and your family. It is the natural state of the world, as we watch the seasons change and the earth producing flowers, fruit, and crops. Although some years are leaner than others, in general Mother Nature provides for the needs of all her dependents—and that includes us.

Living in a state of abundance means you can pay your bills, you have food in the fridge and some savings to fall back on should an unexpected expense arise, such as a car repair. Abundance offers peace of mind. When there is plenty of money in the bank, you don't need to worry as much about the state of the economy, because your own micro-economy is in good health, and you have more than you need.

When you have more than you need, you feel calm and happy. When you have less than you need, you feel fraught and fearful. Developing your own margin of happiness is the key to personal abundance. Prosperity is a personal journey. The amount of money that makes one person feel wealthy might make someone else feel poor.

A lot of it has to do with your comfort levels around money. If you have been struggling to make ends meet, suddenly having $500 might make you feel rich, while for someone who regularly spends thousands of dollars on luxury goods, being down to just $500 might make them feel destitute, so what makes you feel abundant is entirely subjective.

CASTING FOR MONEY AND PROSPERITY

It is an acceptable practice to cast spells for money, but there are a few things to keep in mind. First of all, you should cast money spells based on need, not greed, because the sense of urgency to get your needs met will make the spell more powerful. Casting to win the lottery with the vague notion that you would like to be rich is unlikely to succeed, because there is no genuine emotional need driving the spell. So cast for just a little bit more than you actually need for your margin of happiness.

Money spells can manifest in many ways—overtime at work, a raise, a tax rebate, a windfall. It won't usually be "free money" that comes to you out of the blue, but it will be money that you have either worked for or overpaid. That said,

sometimes a windfall will come to you after a prosperity spell has been cast, and that always feels magical, but it is usually the case that you will need to participate in acquiring additional cash, even with magic on your side.

Because money can sometimes come through negative routes, such as insurance pay-outs and compensation, it is wise to add a simple caveat to all your money spells to ensure that any money coming your way comes through positive means, and with harm to none. So at the end of every spell for abundance you should say:

I cast this spell with harm to none
For the good of all, so it be done

This will ensure that all your prosperity spells work in a nice, gentle manner and via a positive means of manifestation.

HOW MUCH DO YOU NEED?

It is surprising how many people don't actually know how much money they need to live on each month, or how much they spend on non-essentials. This is vital information, and it's the first thing you need to determine before you begin casting money spells. There is no point in casting for more money if you have no clue where your current income is going. If money runs through your fingers like water, you need to find out where it's going. Are you *really* not making enough to live on, or are you simply overspending?

So the first step is to figure out exactly how much money you need every month to pay your bills, keep the car running, and buy groceries. Add up these expenses to come up with a single figure. This is your baseline, your survival money. If your income is below this threshold, you are not making enough money. If it is above, but only by a little bit, you are still in a precarious position. If you have quite a bit more than your baseline, but you're still struggling financially, you are probably overspending and you need to figure out where your frivolous spending zones are. It could be a habit of online shopping, or a tendency to eat at restaurants too often. Find the money drain, and put a plug in it.

Once you have your baseline figure, you can figure out how much you want to start saving for your margin of happiness, or toward a specific event such as a wedding, Christmas funds or a nice vacation. This in turn will determine how much extra money you need to bring in each month, which is the figure you should base your spell-casting around. Alternatively, you can cast for a sum of money to cover the cost of a large purchase, such as a new appliance.

Spell to Make a General Prosperity Pouch

Items required: a green pouch, three silver coins, a lodestone crystal, half a cinnamon stick
Timing: on the new moon

This spell works to keep prosperity flowing toward you at all times. Place the items on your pentacle to charge overnight as the new moon first appears. The next day, hold the coins and the crystal in your hands and say:

Coins of silver shining bright
Bring forth to me by new moon light
The gift of great prosperity
This lodestone draws it here to me
In peace and plenty I will thrive
My increased wealth now comes alive!

money you require. Anoint the candle in patchouli oil, by rubbing the oil from the top to the middle of the candle, then from the bottom to the middle. This will help bring money to you from all directions. Sprinkle a small amount of dried mint on a sheet of paper towel and roll the candle through the herb, pulling it toward you as you do so. Maintain your visualization throughout this process. Finally, place the candle in the holder, light the wick and say the incantation below, then allow the candle to burn out naturally.

Blessings of wealth come hither from there
I call forth abundance to fly through the air
Circle about and surround me with glee
The sum I require now comes to me!

Place the coins and crystal in the pouch, then, using the cinnamon stick, trace a dollar sign on the pouch and put the cinnamon stick inside to draw money to you. Keep this prosperity pouch near you as you sleep, to keep money flowing to you.

Spell for a Specific Sum of Money
Items required: a green candle and holder, athame or carving tool, patchouli oil, dried mint, paper towel
Timing: during new to full moon

If there is something you need a specific sum of money for—say, a vacation, or a special purchase—then cast this spell as the moon waxes from new to full. Visualize what you want the money for and see yourself enjoying it. Take a green candle and carve into the wax the amount of

A Prosperity Bath
Items required: a green pouch or hankie, dried mint, a cinnamon stick, a piece of raw ginger, a few coins, a green ribbon
Timing: use this spell on the night of the full moon

Place the coins in the pouch or the middle of the hankie. Add a teaspoon of dried mint, the cinnamon stick and ginger. These are all associated with prosperity and abundance.

Tie the pouch or hankie into a bundle and hang it from the faucet as you run a bath, letting the water run over the pouch releasing the scents. You can also leave the pouch in the water to infuse if you want to. Enjoy a relaxing bath, soaking in the waters of prosperity. This will cloak you in the energies of abundance and, as like attracts like, you will attract prosperity like a magnet. To keep money flowing toward you, perform this bathing ritual every couple of months or so, and at least once a quarter— that is, every three months.

Grow Your Own Abundance

Items required: a small mint plant, a nice pot, three aventurine crystals
Timing: on the new moon

Mint is one of the most powerful herbs for attracting prosperity, which is why it features in so many money spells. It is also remarkably easy to grow, either in your yard, if you have one, or on a sunny windowsill. Once you have chosen your plant, pot it and put the three aventurine crystals on top of the soil around the base of the plant. This will add to the abundance magic you're creating. Care for the mint, envisioning it bringing wealth and plenty, and as it grows, your sense of abundance should grow with it. This ritual has the added benefit that you can use mint for your money spells and in cooking; it is worth taking the time to grow a pot, so you will always have it handy for your magic.

A Spell for Money Wisdom

Items required: a piece of iron pyrite, also known as fool's gold, a sage smudge bundle and lighter, your wallet or bag, your bank cards, your pentacle

You work hard for your money and put it to good use, but frivolous spending habits can leave you feeling the pinch if you're not careful. Sometimes it's easy to get carried away and spend too much. However, being wise with your money and considering your purchases carefully before you buy anything will lead to a greater sense of prosperity and control

A fool with money I shall not be
No longer spending frivolously
I keep these cards close to my chest
And with prosperity I am blessed

Keep the fool's gold in your bag or wallet to act as a reminder to be more careful with your money.

Magical Tips to Keep the Money Flowing In

- Put a bay leaf in your purse to ensure it is never empty.
- Carry a lodestone in your pocket to keep your pockets full.
- Carry a buckeye to draw natural abundance your way.
- Drink mint tea often to take prosperity into yourself.
- Keep aventurine crystals on your desk at work to increase earnings.
- Put the king and queen of diamonds playing cards in your wallet or purse to guard your wealth.

COPING WITH DEBT

The flip side of prosperity is debt, which can act as a block to your abundance. While not all debt is bad, it can lead to anxiety and stress if you are having trouble keeping up with payments. This includes "good" debts, such as mortgages and student loans.

of your finances. Cast this spell to help you achieve financial wisdom.

Gather your cards and your bag or wallet. Place them on the pentacle, light the smudge bundle and waft the smoke all around the cards and bag to cleanse them of any negative money habits. Imagine having the discipline to only buy essential purchases and to leave stores or close down web browsers without buying anything. Think of what you could do with the money you save simply by being more discerning in your shopping habits. Imagine making wise investments with your money, or having a healthy savings account. Keep smudging your cards as you envision yourself growing in financial wisdom. When you are ready, pick up the fool's gold and say:

In general, consumer debts are the ones most people struggle to manage—things like credit cards. Such debts generally have high interest rates, which means you can find yourself struggling to keep up the payments.

For people on a low income with no savings, debt can be a fact of life. It is usually the only way they can replace a large appliance if it breaks down, or afford to pay an unexpected expense such as vet bills or car problems. But the fact that debt is normal doesn't make it any less stressful, and borrowing on tomorrow's salary to pay for something today is to be avoided at all costs. That's because when the time comes to repay the debt, not only will you need to pay for your basic expenses, you'll also need to pay back the new debt, leaving less money to put into savings and an even smaller margin of happiness.

Debt can also become a habit. It's easy to get into a *treat yourself* mindset, and if you have been working all month it might seem reasonable to purchase something nice as a reward. That's fine, as long as you can afford it, or if you only treat yourself using credit cards every now and then. However, if you are in the habit of going on shopping sprees, then eventually it can lead to money issues, particularly if you are carrying debt from month to month. Also keep in mind that it is beneficial for

credit-card companies to keep you in debt, because they can keep charging interest on what you owe, which is why they might increase your credit limit if you are close to the existing limit.

That said, if you tell a company you're struggling to make payments and are experiencing financial difficulty, they can help you come to a payment agreement you can afford. But if you default on one of these payments, they can demand the balance in full or pass the account to a debt-collection agency, which will add its own fees, increasing your overall debt.

So how do you cope if you are in this kind of situation and your debts are increasing rather than decreasing? First of all, try to automate as many of the payments as you can by setting up direct debits for an agreed amount each month. This takes some of the pressure off you, because you won't need to think about the payments. Next, put your credit cards in a safe place until you're on top of your debts. Keeping them in your bag just keeps temptation handy, and you need to break the habit of acquiring debt. Finally, use the debt-management spells below to put a little magic on your side and regain control of your finances, because paying off your debts is also a way of banishing poverty (but be aware that spells alone will not solve your problems; practical steps will be required too).

Silent Spell to Diminish Debt

Items required: two 2" squares of card, a black pen, black electrical tape
Timing: during a waning moon

You can use this spell in two ways. First, you can add up all the debts you owe to come up with your total amount of debt. Second, you can use the spell for a single creditor, dealing with one debt at a time. Whichever method you choose, write the amount you owe in black pen at the top of one of the squares of card, then copy out the amount, omitting the final digit in each line until you are left with nothing, like this:

$150,000.00
$150,000.0
$150,000
$150,00
$150,0
$150
$15
$1
$0

Once you have written the debt in this way, place the second square of card on top of the first one, to cover the numbers, then use the black tape to wrap around the card until it is fully covered. This will help prevent the debt from increasing. Place the diminishing spell in a dark place, and once the debt is paid, burn it, giving thanks.

A Spell for Desperate Times

Items required: a candle of any color (use whatever you have in the house), a candle holder, black pepper, paper towel, sunflower or any other oil you have handy
Timing: use in times of desperate need

Desperate times call for desperate measures, and this emergency spell is perfect when creditors are hounding you, bailiffs are coming or you need more time to pay an essential bill such as rent, mortgage, or electricity. Hold the candle in your hands and visualize your creditors being understanding and helpful to you, offering a payment plan or giving you more time to pay. This spell is about giving you some breathing space— it won't make the problem go away, so you will need to be brave and communicate with your creditors. However, this spell should turn down the heat somewhat. Once you have visualized a positive resolution, anoint the candle in oil. Sprinkle the black pepper, which has banishing properties, on the kitchen roll and push the candle through the pepper, pushing it away from you to banish the problem. Place the candle in the holder and light it. Allow it to burn for 30 minutes a day until the situation is resolved, which is usually before the candle has burnt to the end.

Spell to Call in a Debt

Items required: *a small mirror, the amount of money that is owed to you written on a slip of paper, your pentacle*
Timing: *new moon*

If someone owes you money, you can use this spell to call in the debt. This spell is helpful to get a large company to pay back money they owe you, or it can be used if you have loaned money to a friend or family member and you need it back. On the night of the full moon, take the items needed to your altar, or to a quiet place. Write down the sum of money that is owed to you, or if you are unsure, write down something like *Return overpayments on my utility bill* along with the name of the company. Set the mirror in the middle of the pentacle and place the piece of paper on top, face down with the amount of money toward the mirror. Now say the following incantation nine times:

> *That which is owed returns to me*
> *It comes with love and grace*

> *That which is owed comes back to me*
> *Reflected through this sacred space.*
> *So be it*

The debt should be repaid within a full lunar phase, so by the following new moon.

Magical Tips to Banish Debt

- Sprinkle black pepper around your house to keep debt from your door.
- Smudge all your bills with sage as they come in to prevent negative energy from attaching to them.
- Pay your bills on a Thursday, the day of Jupiter, to maintain control of your finances.
- Automate as many payments and bills as you can to free up your head space and avoid late-payment fees.
- Magically cleanse your bag and cards once a month using incense or a smudge bundle.
- Hold a rose quartz crystal in your hand when you talk to creditors to ensure a positive outcome and conversation.
- Remember that the main lesson of debt is that it has to be paid back at some stage, so avoid overspending and keep your debts to a minimum.

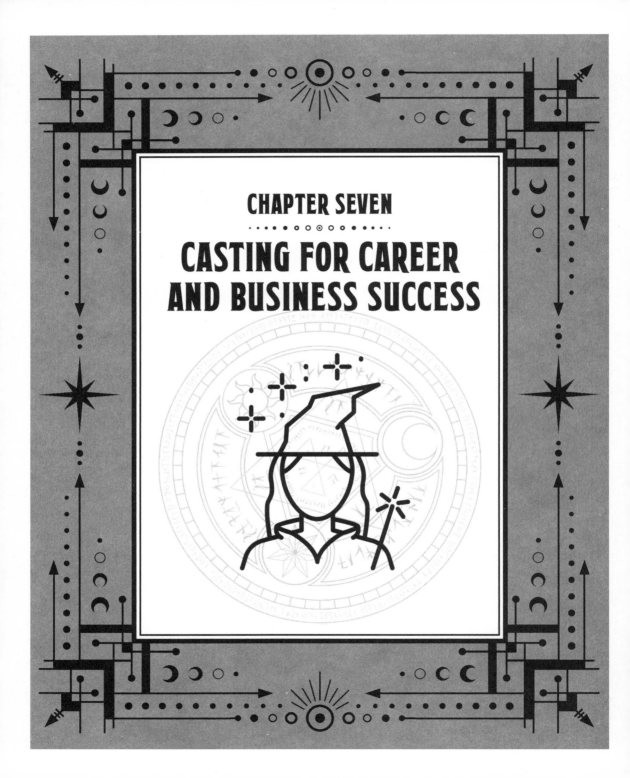

CHAPTER SEVEN

CASTING FOR CAREER AND BUSINESS SUCCESS

You spend approximately one third of your life at work, so it is vital that you enjoy your job as much as possible. Sadly, this isn't always the case, and lots of people feel tied to a job they hate or an employer who expects too much for too little. Unless you are in your dream job, working in a vocation you love, you might only be at work for the money, simply because you have bills to pay. This is certainly the case for many people and, while working for a living is a fact of life, it isn't always easy.

The workplace can often be a cause of stress, anxiety, and depression, with enforced overtime, zero-hours contracts, disgruntled members of the public and difficult colleagues all playing a part in adding to the stress. It isn't easy to create a harmonious team when you have a clash of characters, cultures, and personalities. All workplaces bring together very different people who are expected to merge as one and work as a team, but this can sometimes be challenging.

In an ideal world, everyone would get along and work together toward a common goal, but this isn't always the case. It is inevitable that at some stage in your career you will be forced to work with someone you don't like or can't get along with. It is likely that you'll have to work alongside someone who doesn't pull their weight or do their fair share, leaving you to pick up the slack. If you are a woman working in a male-dominated environment, or vice versa, you might feel that you have to work twice as hard to prove you are worthy of the job. Add to this the fact that employment contracts are usually skewed in the employer's favor, leaving the employee at a disadvantage, and it's not surprising that workplace stress is one of the leading causes of sickness and absenteeism.

In this chapter, we will look at what you can do magically to make your work life more enjoyable, including how you can leave a job you hate, get a promotion, or start a side business.

Spell to Transition from a Bad Job to a Dream Job

Items required: a notebook and pen, a black candle, athame or carving tool, a white candle, two plates, black pepper and white rice
Timing: on the full moon

It can be debilitating when you feel trapped in a job you dislike. However, leaving might not be an option until you've found something else, so use this spell to make that transition easier. Write down what you want from your ideal job, from the hours and salary to the kind of colleagues you prefer to work with. Next carve the words My Dream Job on the white candle and your current job on the black candle. Set the candles on the plates, melting the bottoms so they stand securely. Put the plates side by side. Sprinkle a circle of black pepper around the black candle to banish the negative influence of your current job, then sprinkle a circle of white rice for prosperity around the white candle to help manifest your dream job. Light the black candle and say:

My work is done within this place
My time here will soon be done
I walk away with joy and grace
Happy to be moving on!

Spend a few minutes visualizing your final day at your current job, with all your colleagues wishing you well in the future. When you can see this clearly, light the white candle and say:

I summon my dream job to me
In a role that I enjoy
I call this opportunity
With the magic I now deploy

Finally, burn the slip of paper describing your dream job in the flame of the white candle. You can begin the transition by job hunting and seeking out new opportunities, but this spell should work within six months.

Silent Spell to Shine in an Interview

Items required: a pentacle, a small item that you will wear to the interview, a citrine

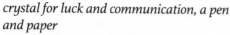

crystal for luck and communication, a pen and paper
Timing: *the day before the interview*

Job interviews can be nerve-wracking and overwhelming. Preparation is the key to success, and the more interviews you do, the more comfortable you will be. Research the company you're interviewing with; they will usually ask you if you know anything about them. At least look at their website and pick up key phrases and mission statements that you can use as part of your interview strategy. It's also a good idea to have a couple of examples from your current or previous work, to demonstrate times when you went above and beyond your role, or when you feel you could have done better and what you would do differently. Once you're prepared, you're ready to cast the spell. Take a small item that you plan to wear to the interview, such as a tie or a piece of jewelry, and place it on the pentacle. Add the crystal. On a slip of paper, write out the following charm:

> *Gracious, kind and sharp of mind*
> *Success in my job interview I find*

Put this paper beneath the crystal and memorize the words so you can mentally affirm them on the way to the interview and while you're waiting to be called in.

This will keep your mind active and your emotions positive. Leave all the items in place overnight to charge on the pentacle. The following day, as you get ready, put on the jewelry or tie and see yourself conducting a great interview. Finally, put the slip of paper and the crystal in your bag, to carry the magic with you. If you get the job, burn the paper and give thanks. If not, keep the spell in place on the pentacle and use it for future interviews; there's probably something better coming.

Spell to Cope with Difficult Colleagues

Items required: *an amethyst crystal or amethyst jewelry, a bottle of spring water*
Timing: *on the waning moon and then whenever you have to work with a difficult colleague, daily if needed*

same purpose—pour a cup of water and place it between you and the person you find challenging to work with. The water will help absorb their negative energy. Just make sure you don't drink it! Pour it away or wash the crystal under running water at the end of each work day.

Spell to Sweeten Up a Difficult Boss

Items required: a small spell jar and stopper, a small slip of paper and a pen, sugar
Timing: at the new moon

No matter how kind and patient you are, there will be times when a colleague gets on your nerves. Maybe they never stop talking and you need to try and concentrate through their verbal diarrhea, or perhaps they are trying to lure you into gossip and office politics. Maybe they're lazy, and you are tired of doing their job as well as your own. Whatever the issue, use this simple spell to absorb their negative energy before it can bring you down. Take the amethyst crystal and let it sit in the light of the waning moon. You can also use a power bracelet of amethyst beads. Allow it to charge until the moon is dark, then take the crystals to work with you and place them between you and the difficult colleague, or keep them on you, to absorb any negative energy coming your way. If a crystal is too obviously out of place on your desk, use the bottled water for the

Putting someone's name in sugar is a traditional folk spell used to bring out their sweeter nature. If you have to work with a difficult boss, it can be hard to stand up for yourself for fear of losing your job. Keep in mind that things like sexual harassment and workplace bullying should always be reported to your manager (or above). If your boss is simply grumpy, irritable, or impatient, however, then try this spell to sweeten them up. Write their name on a piece of paper, roll it up, and place it in the spell jar, then fill the jar with sugar. Put on the stopper and keep the jar safe at home, where it won't be discovered by nosy colleagues!

Spell for a Raise or Promotion

Items required: an envelope, a green pen, three leaves of fresh mint, a sprig of

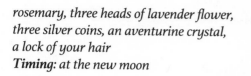

rosemary, three heads of lavender flower, three silver coins, an aventurine crystal, a lock of your hair
***Timing:** at the new moon*

Often, a promotion comes with greater responsibility, so make sure this is what you want before you cast a spell. To bring about a raise, a promotion, or both, take the envelope and write the new job title and salary you are aiming for on the inside of the flap using the green pen. Next, fill the envelope with the following: aventurine and mint for prosperity, lavender for luck, rosemary for growth and success, and three silver coins to increase your pay. Add the lock of hair, seal the envelope and say:

> *Time to shine and room to grow*
> *Greater success I wish to know*
> *A promotion sealed within this place*
> *It comes to me through time and space*
> *By earth, moon and sun*
> *By magic it is done*

Once you have been given a raise or promotion, empty the contents of the envelope into the ground, keeping the coins for future prosperity spells. Give thanks for the new role by burning incense and dedicating it to your chosen deity.

Spell for a Successful Business Venture

***Items required:** a green candle and holder, a few sunflower seeds, the name of your business or creative venture written down*
***Timing:** during a waxing moon*

Lots of people like to have a side business alongside their main job. Not only can it provide additional income, it can also offer relief from your normal job, giving you something else to focus on. Developing a side business has never been easier, and you can set up shop online with little expense. All you need to do is figure out what kind of business you want to create. Then write it down and place the paper beneath a green candle. Light the candle and place two or three sunflower seeds around the candle holder to signify the growth of your business venture. Light the candle and say:

> *With this light I find my way*
> *To make my passion bear fruit*
> *I start this venture from today*
> *And for the stars I'll shoot!*

Allow the candle to burn down naturally and then plant the sunflower seeds. These are the seeds of your dreams, so tend them carefully as you go about making your business idea a reality. Good luck!

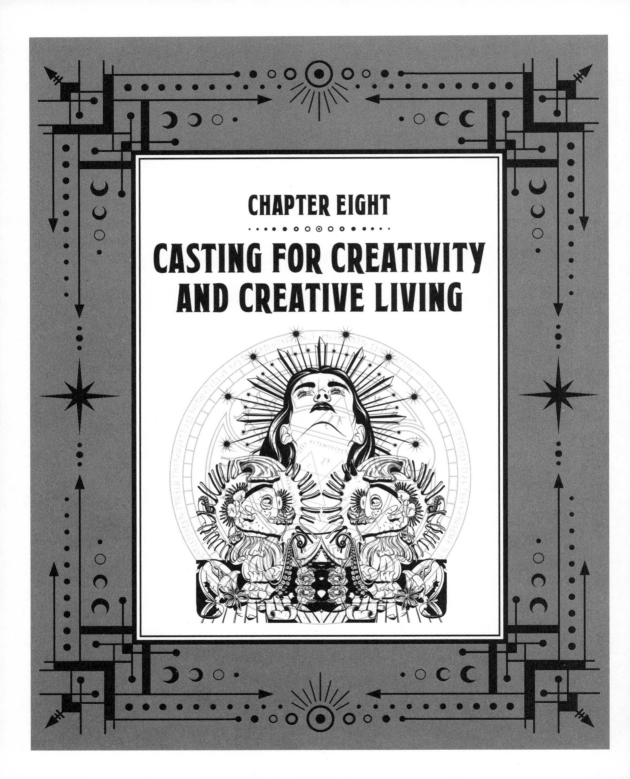

CHAPTER EIGHT

CASTING FOR CREATIVITY AND CREATIVE LIVING

It has never been easier to live a creative life. There are many ways to be creative and many different platforms through which you can share your work with the world. From video channels to podcasts and web sites, you can create something in the comfort of your own home and quickly share it with a global audience.

This way of living is still relatively new; some people aren't sure what to make of it all. But the need to be creative is as old as the hills, and we all feel it in some way. Whether your talent lies in baking, needlework, pottery, music, art, dance, writing, singing, or something else, the spells in this chapter will help you hone your skills and make creativity a natural aspect of your everyday life.

CREATIVE LIVING

Living a creative life comes easily to many people, and it is very rewarding. Whether you intend to share your work in a professional capacity at some stage or not, creating something from nothing is still a pleasurable experience. Having hobbies such as sketching, knitting, writing, and so on offers a way to calm the mind in times of stress. Lots of creative pastimes involve working with the hands, giving the mind a chance to switch off completely.

In the past, women would spend their time spinning wool into yarn, sitting at the spinning wheel for hours on end, chatting and bonding through shared labor. The term *spinster*, meaning a single woman, comes from this traditionally female craft. The menfolk would work with wood or metal, mending fences and making homes ready for the winter. We can still see echoes of this in modern life, as people happily sit knitting together, making garments, while others retreat to their garden or workshop.

So creativity is just as much a part of modern life as it has always been, and there are endless ways to incorporate creative interests into your life. Once you find a hobby you love, you will probably never look back.

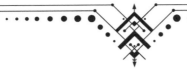

Ritual to Bless Your Creative Space

Items required: rose water, a little salt, a chalice
Timing: each new moon

Take the items to the area where you usually work on your creative projects. Pour some rose water into the chalice and add a little of the salt. Swirl the chalice to help the salt dissolve. You can use this mixture to consecrate your space, allowing the salt to cleanse the area as the rose water purifies and brings positive energies. Moving in a clockwise direction, dip into the chalice and sprinkle the mixture from your fingertips all around your work area and the tools you use, saying:

> *Spirit of rose which blooms and grows*
> *Let my creativity flow*
> *As each petal opens brightly*
> *I will not take my talent lightly*
> *I hone my skills, my talent blooms*
> *Whenever I work within this room*
> *So mote it be*

Blessing Jar for Inspiration

Items required: a large jar and lid, a small notepad and pen, your favorite incense
Timing: begin on the dark moon

It always seems to be when you are in the middle of a project that lots of new

ideas keep bubbling up in your mind. Just because you don't have time to work on them immediately doesn't mean you shouldn't honor these ideas. In this ritual, you will create a sacred space in which to keep each idea as it comes up. First cleanse the jar, inside and out, using the smoke from the incense stick. Hold the jar in your hands and say:

> *May this jar keep safe and bless all my ideas until I am ready to work on them*

When a new idea comes to you, write it down, tear off and fold the note and drop it into the jar. This will ensure that you always have plenty of ideas to fall back on when you need them. Simply take one from the jar and begin.

Ritual for Starting a Creative Session

Items required: a white candle and holder, frankincense essential oil and an oil burner, a cup of your favorite tea, some snacks
Timing: whenever you're about to get creative

Sometimes, getting started can be the hardest part, so add a little magic to make it easier. Atmospheres are a kind of magic, and creating the right one is a ritual in itself. To make the atmosphere conducive to creativity, you need to make sure your space is warm and comfortable, since you might be working on a project for hours at a time. To begin, burn a few drops of frankincense essential oil in an oil burner, or sprinkle it onto a hankie and place it on a radiator near your workspace. Frankincense is good for aiding concentration and creativity. It has a warm scent that can be very comforting. Next, light the candle and place it nearby so it casts a glow over your work. Finally, ensure that you have your favorite snacks and a drink handy, so that you don't have to keep going to the kitchen. When everything is ready, settle into your space and say:

Golden hours of creative time
Offer me a chance to shine
A project here before me lies
As I work hard the time flies
Beat by beat of a creative heart

The project grows, which now I start
So it begins...

Get your head down and start working! This ritual helps get you into the right mind-set for creative work, and is useful for academic essays as well as creative projects.

Silent Seven-Day Spell for Successful Creativity

Items required: a tall orange candle and holder, athame or carving tool, a citrine crystal
Timing: during the seven days leading to full moon

This spell can be used to help support a new project you want to work on. Take the orange candle and carve something that represents your creative goal—for instance, the word "author." Put the candle in the holder and place the citrine crystal in front. Citrine is a crystal of communication, and all forms of creativity are essentially a way of communicating with ourselves and with others. Light the candle and hold your hands on either side, palms facing. Imagine the success of your creative project and see yourself enjoying that success—for instance, your book being published, your paintings being exhibited, your audition going well,

or being invited to join a dance company. Wherever your creativity is aimed, see yourself reaching that target. Visualize this for a while, then let the candle burn a seventh of the way down. Extinguish the candle and repeat the process for the next six days. On the final day, let the candle burn all the way out. Keep the citrine crystal with you as you work on your project.

Dandelion Spell for Creative Growth

Items required: six dandelion flowers, a tea-light and holder, something to represent your creative interest
Timing: during a full moon

The humble dandelion has been much maligned by gardeners, often viewed as nothing more than a weed and treated accordingly. But try as they might, the little flower always makes a comeback. What's more, it has many magical properties, and is frequently used in herbal remedies and healing spells. The dandelion also has planetary associations, because it represents both the sun and the moon, first with its bright golden head, then later with its downy white orb. Thus it became known as a plant of abundant growth and self-transformation. For this spell you will need six dandelion flowers. Place them in a circle around the tea-light. Light the candle, focus on the item you have chosen to represent your creative goal, and imagine living that life. Now say:

Precious bloom of golden hue
I seek out my golden days
To find transformation in what I do
When I am at play
Let my talent grow and yield
Brighter days ahead
Transforming the dream that I wield
Into reality instead.

Let the tea-light burn as you work, then press the flowers and use them to decorate your creative space, keeping the magic they hold linked to your creativity.

Spell to Manifest a Large Creative Goal

Items required: a sheet of paper, a golden ribbon, frankincense essential oil, a lodestone crystal
Timing: on the new moon

If you're planning a large creative project, such as writing a book, this spell can help keep you on track. It is a type of scribe spell, so you will need to write down what your project is and why you want to do it. What are your motivations? Do you plan to share it with an audience, or is it something you're doing for your own enjoyment? Be clear about why you want to make time for this hobby and what you hope to gain from it. Once you have it all written down, read through it to make sure it encapsulates your intentions clearly. Anoint the ribbon with a couple of drops of frankincense oil, then roll the paper up into a scroll and tie it with the ribbon. Kiss the scroll and say:

> *Here where my intention lies*
> *A charm is made for dreams to thrive*
> *A kiss to send them on their way*
> *To manifest some future day*
> *From this day forth I will go on*
> *Working until the job is done*

Place the scroll in a place where you'll see it every day and put the lodestone next to it to magnetize the completion of the project. Make time for your hobby each day, and watch the project grow to completion.

Spell to Invoke Your Muse

Items required: a bell or wind chimes, sandalwood incense
Timing: whenever you need a bit of extra help with your creativity

Go to your creative space and take three deep breaths. Light the incense and waft it around the area to cleanse, then place it on your desk and say: *I offer this incense to my muse.* Next, take the bell or chimes and ring them in all four directions: north, south, east, and west. After each ring, say:

*Angel of creativity I call you here to
    assist me
Light of inspiration, burning bright
Wings of genius taking flight
Sacred Muse I summon you from far
    or near
Come to me now and settle here.*

Begin your work and know that your muse guides your hands and thoughts, bringing your dreams into being.

Ritual to Grow Your Own Creative Dream

Items required: a shallow pan or seed tray, potting soil, water, watercress seeds, athame
Timing: when the moon is new

To nurture the seeds of your dreams, transport them out of your mind and into reality. Hold a packet of watercress seeds in your hands and imagine your creative goal. Visualize that goal being absorbed by the seeds, and think of a single word that sums it up. Put a layer of potting soil in the tray and level it out. Next, use the athame to trace the word in the soil, then sow the seeds along the channel of the word. Cover with another layer of potting soil, making sure not to destroy the word you have just written. Water the seeds and place them on a sunny windowsill to grow.

Then eat the watercress to take the success of the magic into yourself. Make sure you are living intentionally and taking positive steps toward your creative dream.

Genius Burns Spell

Items required: a lantern, tea-lights
Timing: whenever you are inspired to work creatively

A perpetual flame is a way of keeping magic flowing, and of honoring something. In this spell, we honor the idea of a perpetual flame but use it in a safe way to help ideas flow. You will need a lantern designed to hold tea-lights, and a good supply of them. Keep the lantern on your desk as you work, lighting a candle in it each time you settle down to your project and saying:

If genius burns within me
Let me feels its flame
If a work of art shall shape me
Help me embrace the fame
This light that burns within
Now shines for all to see
Let the flow begin
As bright ideas burn through me

Dreaming Spell to Find Your Creative Passion

Items required: lavender pillow spray, nine stems of lavender, a purple ribbon
Timing: anytime from new to full moon

Your dreams are meant to guide you, and highlight your potential. They can show you all you can be if you trust the process and listen to your intuition. This dream spell is designed to help you uncover where your creative talents lie. If you think you have no talent, think again—everyone has a gift of some kind, and you just need to figure out what yours is. Lavender is well known for its power to induce sleep and relaxation. It can also help you get in touch with your intuition through the power of your dreams. Just before you go to bed, use the pillow spray generously. Now make a posy of the lavender stems by picking them up one at a time and saying the appropriate line of the charm below:

By stem of one the dream is begun
By stem of two the dream comes true
By stem of three so shall it be
By stem of four the dream shows me more
By stem of five the dream comes alive
By stem of six the dream is not fixed
By stem of seven and all stars in heaven
By stem of eight the dream holds weight
By stem of nine, the dream comes tonight

Tie the dream posy with the ribbon and hang it upside down from your bed post, or place it on your bedside table with the flowers pointing toward you. Pay attention to your dreams over the next few nights to gain insight into where your talent lies and

which ambition you should follow.

Wax Talisman to Open Doors to Your Chosen Creative Industry

Items required: gold sealing wax, baking parchment, a fresh three- or four-leaf clover
Timing: cast on the full moon for greatest power

Carrying a talisman with you can ensure that you find yourself in the right place at the right time. It can open doors for you and lead you to the right people. This talisman is created to steer you closer to your creative industry, be it publishing, theatre, music, or whatever. Sometimes all you need is a lucky break, and a talisman is one way to give yourself the best chance of a breakthrough. Lay out a square of baking parchment. Light the stick of sealing wax and allow it to drip onto the paper until you have a pool of wax about the size of the base of a tealight. Then take the clover leaf and press it gently into the wax. Leave it to dry thoroughly, then gently peel it off the greaseproof paper. Carry the wax talisman with you at all times to bring about the best results.

Mirror Spell to Pass an Audition

Items required: a small compact mirror, a white pouch, clear quartz, carnelian and rose quartz crystals, the fragrance you intend to wear for the audition
Timing: one week before the audition

Auditions are an important part of many creative industries, so if your ambition is to act, sing, model, or dance, you will have to learn to be comfortable attending them. They can be nerve-wracking, because you can usually see exactly who the competition is, and rejection might take place face to face. To give yourself the best chance, make sure you're prepared in both appearance and performance. Then boost your chances with this spell. Look into a mirror and say *This is what a successful ballerina (or whatever) looks like. I am a successful ballerina, and great opportunities will come to me.*

Next, spray a little fragrance on the pouch, then put in the following crystals: clear quartz to amplify your performance, carnelian for success, and rose quartz to make those in power look on you with favor. Leave these items to soak up the light of the sun and moon for a week, then take them with you to the audition. Be sure to wear the same fragrance and, just before you go in, look into the mirror and mentally repeat the success charm. While you might not always get the part you want, this spell will ensure that you are given a chance to show what you can do, so don't waste it.

Spell to Break Through Creative Blocks

Items required: a black candle and holder, a carving tool, a strand of your hair, a lighter
Timing: from full to dark moon

Creative blocks happen to the best of us at times, leaving us out of ideas and out of motivation to create. Often people become blocked just after a project has been going well; it can feel as if you've used up all your creative juices and have nothing left to give. This can be frustrating and annoying, particularly if you have a deadline to meet. All is not lost, however; it could just be that you need to sweep away the block with a touch of magic. Carve your name and the nature of the blocked project into the candle, then heat the side of the wax using the lighter and wind the strand of hair around it while the wax is warm enough for it to stick in place. Put the candle in the holder and light the wick as you say:

Creative blocks are cleared away
Let talent thrive another day
In peace and calm I find my way
Back to productivity

Allow the candle to burn for one hour each day, and by the time it has burnt away, the creative block should have passed.

CHAPTER NINE

CASTING FOR PROTECTION

In an ideal world, we would have no need of protection magic. You could leave your handbag on the car seat beside you without worry. However, we do not live in an ideal world and day-to-day life can be scary at times.

We can use protection magic to deal with the darker aspects of life, as a preventative measure. Witches don't wait until their home is burglarized to cast spells to protect it—we cast daily spells to ensure that we are less likely to be targeted.

Protection spells tend to be layered up over time. Prevention is better than cure, so don't wait until something bad happens. Start to cast protection magic now to surround yourself and your property with positive magic. In this chapter you will find all kinds of protection spells, so that you can begin to weave a web of good magic around all that you hold dear.

It is vital that you learn to be your own backup. If you wait around for someone else to fight your battles, you will start to believe that you are incapable of standing up for yourself—and that simply isn't true. Furthermore, you are the *only* person who is always guaranteed to be right there whenever conflict presents itself, so it makes sense to rely on yourself to resolve conflict.

BE YOUR OWN BACKUP

There may be occasions when you find yourself in the wrong place at the wrong time; perhaps you are caught up as a witness in a crime, or you are drawn into an altercation of some kind. Difficult neighbors, a bullying boss, or back-stabbing friends are all situations you might suddenly find yourself embroiled in.

ENGAGE YOUR WARRIOR SPIRIT

The warrior spirit is something we all have inside us. It is the ability to stand firm in the face of adversity, take a well-calculated risk, and develop a plan of action to see a hostile situation through to a peaceful conclusion. It is the power to safeguard loved ones and those who are vulnerable, such as children and animals.

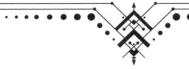

Witches are in tune with their warrior aspect and have the skills of spell-craft at their fingertips. This isn't about looking for trouble. It is about knowing that you have the capability to deal with trouble if and when it presents itself to you. Use the blessing below to evoke your warrior spirit.

Blessing to Evoke Your Warrior Spirit

Items required: a black candle, an essential oil of your choice
Timing: whenever you encounter conflict

Anoint the candle with the oil. As you do so, imagine yourself standing your ground, stating your case firmly and with conviction. See the battleground of conflict before you in your mind's eye. Know that you have what it takes to achieve peace and/or victory. Now light the candle and say the following evocation to summon your warrior spirit.

> *As conflict now presents itself, so I will engage*
> *I stand upon a battle ground and feel the battle rage*
> *I evoke my warrior spirit side to vanquish every foe*
> *To show my wrath till peace be gained, for victory is all I know*

Let the candle burn as you come up with a plan of action to settle the conflict. Then blow out the candle. Embrace your warrior spirit and live your life with courage, confidence, wisdom, and compassion.

Silent Spell to Protect Yourself

Items required: a good-luck charm or magical necklace such as a pentacle or triquetra, altar pentacle
Timing: on the full moon

Wearing a protective charm is a traditional way to ward off negative energy. On the night of the full moon, put the pendent or charm in the middle of the altar pentacle and place it where it can absorb the light of the moon. Leave it overnight, then wear it as your everyday necklace, or carry the charm in your wallet. The charm can help ward away bad vibes in general, but if you feel that you are under threat, move on to the next step below.

Cast a Circle of Personal Protection

Items required: none
Timing: whenever you are feeling vulnerable

Think of this circle as a magical force field that nothing harmful can penetrate. This is a visualization exercise, so you can use it any time, in any situation. Simply envision

a circle of light that expands up over your head and beneath your feet, creating a sphere of magical protection. This circle goes where you go and encompasses all your movements.

Cast this spell regularly, because practice makes it stronger and more effective. You will also notice that people tend to walk around your circle—they can't see it, but they can feel its energy and they will often adjust their steps to avoid crossing the line you have created with your magical boundary. Take this as proof of its power to protect you.

Charm to Protect Your Car

Items required: tiger's eye, hematite and smoky quartz crystals, a small pouch, bergamot essential oil
Timing: at midnight, the witching hour, when the moon is dark

Take the pouch and scent it with the bergamot oil, which is known for its protective powers. Next add the protection crystals. Hold the pouch of crystals in your hands and say:

Protect this vehicle and all within
By the power of this charm herein

Leave the pouch and oil on your altar overnight. The next day place the pouch in the glove compartment of your car and use a little of the oil to anoint each of the tires, both bumpers and the roof. This will seal and complete the spell.

Blessing for Protection When Driving

Items required: Bach Rescue Remedy spray
Timing: use whenever you feel anxious while driving

Driving in traffic can lead to anxiety, so it is a good idea to keep Rescue Remedy spray in your car. This is an herbal remedy for anxiety, stress and nervous disorders. If you are starting to feel a little overwhelmed while driving, or even at the thought of driving, then spray a little Rescue Remedy on your tongue and repeat this blessing.

Sharpen mind and restore wit
To anxiety I'll not submit
East, south, west, north
Angels protect me as I drive back and
*   forth*

This spell can also be used if you are about to embark on a long journey on public transportation.

Spell to Protect Your Property

Items required: *four black stones or pebbles, black pepper, a compass*
Timing: *at dusk on a waning moon*

This spell is designed to create a magical boundary around the perimeter of your property. As dusk falls, go into your yard and use the compass to determine where north lies. Head in that direction to the perimeter of your yard and put down one of the black stones. Now move to the east, sprinkling a little black pepper as you go, and place another stone at the eastern border. Repeat for south and west, sprinkling the black pepper to create a circle, all joined with the boundary stones at each compass point. Continue back to the point where you started, and say:

> *The boundary lines have now been*
> *   cast*
> *With protection magic built to last*

Check that your stones are in place every month. If not, repeat the spell with new stones. If you live in an apartment building, adjust this spell by placing the stones at the compass points inside your apartment, but don't use the pepper.

Silent Spell to Protect a Loved One

Items required: *a small spell jar and stopper, a lock of your loved one's hair, protective dried herbs of basil, sage, and rosemary, a small slip of paper and a pen, black sealing wax, a holly leaf, red thread*
Timing: *on the full moon for strongest protection*

Cast this spell to keep your loved one safe from harm. Write their full name and date of birth on the slip of paper, roll it up and

drop it into the jar. Add the lock of hair. Now fill the jar with the dried herbs, put the stopper in and seal it with black wax. Once the wax has hardened, tie the holly leaf around the neck using the red thread and place the jar in the light of the moon for a full lunar cycle. Then place the jar in a dark corner where it will remain undisturbed.

Rowan Spell to Guard Against Prowlers

Items required: two twigs of rowan, red thread, red ribbon to hang
Timing: at the time of the dark moon

In this ritual, you are going to make a traditional charm that is said to guard against human prowlers and unwelcome visitors from the spirit realms. Make the two rowan twigs into an equal-armed cross and secure with the red thread. Use the red ribbon to hang the charm on or close to your property.

Spell to Protect Against Envious People

Items required: dried rowan berries, black thread, a needle
Timing: cast at midnight during the full moon

Envy is a poison that can have a harmful effect. If someone is showing signs of envy toward you, then you have every right to guard yourself against any spite that might be coming your way. Thread the needle with a long length of black cotton and knot the end. Now begin to thread the rowan berries onto the cotton to create a strand. As you put the needle through each one say:

> *I prick the conscience of those who act and speak against me*
> *For envy touches me not*

Keep going until the thread is full of berries, then tie off the strand. The next day, bury this strand of berries in the ground to help neutralize the envy directed at you. Rowan berries are harmful to pets and can have an adverse effect on people too, so be sure

to bury the strand deep, keep any leftover berries out of reach and wash your hands thoroughly after working with them.

Blessing to Protect Against Storms and Bad Weather

Items required: a white candle or tea-light and holder
Timing: perform as the storm rolls in

We are experiencing more extreme weather than ever before. Floods, high winds and snowstorms can be a danger to life and property, so they are not to be taken lightly. When a storm is forecast, wait until you notice the first signs, then light the candle in the holder and say:

> *Elemental spirits of this storm, I light*
> *   this candle to honor and respect you*
> *I ask that you pass swiftly over the*
> *   homes and property of myself and*
> *   my loved ones*
> *Leaving me and my family unscathed*
> *   in your wake*
> *So mote it be*

If you are at work or out and about when the storm comes, use a lighter to the same effect, letting the flame burn for a few moments as you speak the words of blessing above.

Spell to Protect a Pet

Items required: some of your pet's naturally shed fur, a square of paper, a pen, sealing wax
Timing: from new to full moon

Our pets are members of our family and they deserve just as much protection as any of our loved ones. One of the best things you can do for your pet is get it microchipped, so that if the worst happens, you will be more likely to be reunited. In addition, cast this spell to add a little magical protection around your four-legged friend. On the square of paper write your pet's name in the center, then write the words *Protected Be* on all four sides, surrounding the name. Place your pet's fur in the middle of the paper and fold each corner of the paper into the middle,

then secure it with sealing wax. Keep the protection charm in a safe place.

THE EVIL EYE

Many cultures still believe in the Evil Eye, which is the belief that some people can cause harm and chaos simply by glaring at their chosen victim. While this might seem a little far-fetched, most myths and legends have a basis in fact, and it could be that the Evil Eye legend was a way of explaining extreme spitefulness or vindictive behavior. In certain parts of Europe and in Mediterranean regions, special charms are still sold that are thought to ward off the negative effects of the Evil Eye. These charms look like little eyes, usually blue and white. They work by drawing negative energy into the eye and away from the wearer. Such charms were

also painted on doors and houses, to ward against passing evil. Use the spells below to guard against negative energy.

Spell to Guard Against the Evil Eye
Items required: a lapis lazuli crystal necklace, a pebble, black, blue and white paint, clear varnish
Timing: during the waning moon to draw the negativity away from you

First draw or paint the image of a blue eye on the pebble. Use images of traditional evil-eye charms on the internet to inspire you. Once the paint has dried, add a coat of clear varnish to protect it. Leave the evil eye and the lapis lazuli in the light of the moon for a full lunar phase, then wear the necklace and carry the charmed pebble with you, to draw away all negative energies heading your way.

Spell to Deflect Ill Wishes
Items required: a mirror, or your dominant hand
Timing: use whenever someone is sending spite or ill wishes your way

If you feel that someone is being spiteful toward you, here is a trick you can use to send their bad energy straight back to them. Ideally you would use a small compact mirror, but this isn't always possible, so

you can use your dominant hand instead. Next time someone throws spite in your direction or verbally attacks you, wait until they walk away then simply reject their bad energy by holding up the mirror or your hand toward their back and saying:

Deflected, rejected, returned times three, times three, times three again
May your negativity surround only you

Fire and Brimstone Spell to See Off Your Enemies

Items required: a box of matches, a cauldron or ashtray
Timing: on a waning moon

Sulfur has been used in protection spells for centuries. Also known as brimstone, it is a staple in the witch's magical cabinet, usually in the form of matches. Matches are an easy and accessible way to use sulfur in your spells, so it's a good idea to keep a box handy. Place your empty cauldron in front of you and the box of matches on your lap. Take out a match and name it for the *actions* of your enemy, for example:

I name this match for those who try to sabotage my career
Let their vendetta against me burn out with it

Strike the match and watch it burn, then drop it into the cauldron just before the flame reaches your fingers and say:

Ashes to ashes and dust to dust

Repeat with as many matches as it takes until you feel the magic *pop*. This is usually a feeling of energy released from the solar plexus area of your body, followed by a feeling of euphoria. Know that the magic is in play and your enemy should move on within a month.

Spell to Protect Your Interests

Items required: a small cardboard box such as a matchbox, the issue that is under threat written on a slip of paper, dried herbs of rosemary and basil for protection, a length of bramble, a thistle, gardening gloves

Timing: at the time of the waning moon

This is a great spell to defend yourself against the back-stabbers of the world. They might be trying to sabotage your business, undermine you at work, steal your job or your partner, or tarnish your reputation. Whatever the nature of this attack is, write it down on a slip of paper as soon as you become aware of it. Sign and date the paper, then put it in the box and add the herbs until the box is full. Put on the gardening gloves and wind the bramble around the box, twisting the stem so that it is securely in place. Weave a thistle into the bramble on top of the box. Place it in the light of the waning moon and say:

You cannot touch me, you cannot
*   harm me*

You cannot take what's mine
You cannot scare me, you cannot
*   diminish me*
You cannot destroy what's mine
You cannot stop me, you cannot beat
*   me*
For if you even try
By sharpest thorn and vengeful thistle
This magic will reply!

Keep the spell box in a safe place, maybe near your altar. Know that if someone moves against you and your success, they will only bring upon themselves the retribution of your spell, via the threefold law.

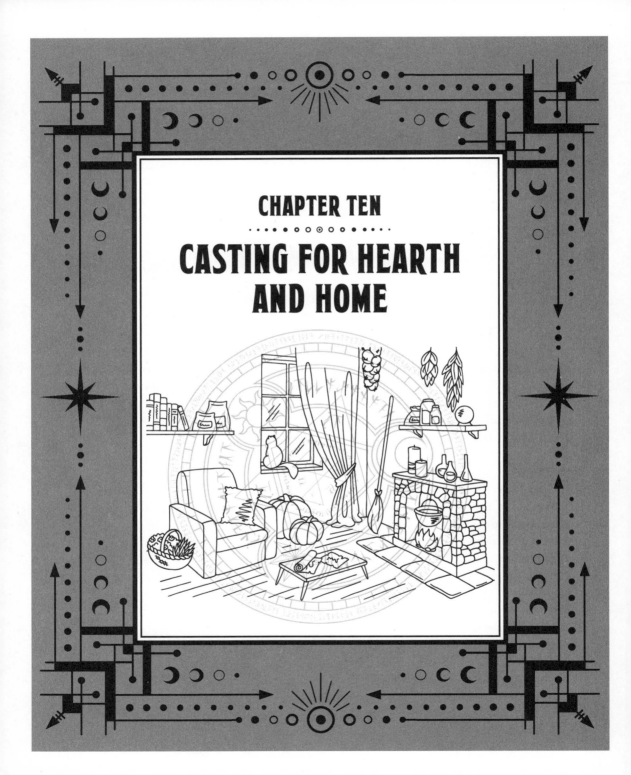

CHAPTER TEN

CASTING FOR HEARTH AND HOME

Your home should feel like the safest place in the world. Whether it's a studio apartment or a mansion, it's your space, and it should serve as a welcome retreat from the world. A home is a place of cozy comfort and restoration, somewhere to relax, recharge, and close out the rest of society if you choose. It should be a place of freedom of expression, where you can speak your mind and display your personality in the decor and the things you have around you. It could also be somewhere that you throw open the doors to welcome friends and neighbors, in the spirit of congeniality.

While few people are fortunate enough to live in a fairy-tale cottage on the edge of a forest or by the sea, you can still bring an element of witchy enchantment into your home. Witches have always placed charms on their homes, for protection, relaxation, harmony, hospitality, and many other things. But a witch's house is always imbued with magical energy. Visitors often pick up on this energy, commenting on how relaxed they feel and how the house has a lovely atmosphere. Often, they can't wait to come back for another visit; they might even try to achieve the same atmosphere in their own homes.

You can create this kind of magical atmosphere too, using the spells in this chapter to cast an air of charm and enchantment around your place, however grand or humble it might be.

THE HEARTH WITCH

A hearth witch is a magical practitioner who works in solitude from the comfort of her own home. Hearth witches are usually concerned with local issues and concentrate mainly on creating a safe and magical home for themselves and their families. They tend to cast simple spells using ingredients that can be found around the house or purchased easily. Hearth witchery is a type of folk magic, and the spells in this book fall into that category in that they do not involve high-ritual magic. The spells in this chapter will help you turn your home into a magical haven, and a refuge from the stresses and strains of everyday life. In using them, you can begin to turn your own home into a modern version of the fabled witch's cottage.

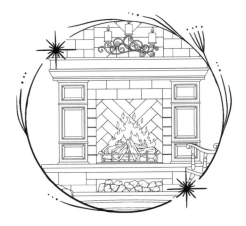

THE MAGICAL HEARTH

The hearth, or fireplace, is the heart of the home. In the past it was where huge fires blazed to keep out the winter cold, and where a great cauldron hung, cooking food for family and guests. Nowadays not all homes have a fireplace. But it is nice to recreate the hearth, if you can, using a stove or a collection of candles. If you do have a fireplace and a mantelpiece, try to make it the focal point of the room, arranging crystals, candles, and ornaments to represent your magical life and personal interests. The hearth is associated with the goddess Bride or Bridget, and as such it should be swept clean, with a fresh candle lit every day to honor her and encourage her blessings to fall upon the house. Tea-lights work best for this, as you can easily burn one each evening. If you have a working fireplace, you should not let the ashes accumulate, as that will draw poverty and hardship to the home. Keep it clean, and the use the blessing below.

Bride's Blessing of the Hearth and Home

Items required: a stick of your favorite incense and holder, two white candles and holders
Timing: each new moon, and on the festival of Imbolc (St Brigid's Day), February 2nd

When you have cleaned your fireplace and dusted the mantelpiece, arrange your candles on either side of the hearth or mantel. Light them, and then light the incense. Wave the smoke around the hearth to bless it and say:

I call Bride's blessings here this day
To guard this place and keep ill at bay

Place the stick in an incense holder and allow it to burn in dedication to Bride and her powers of hearth and home.

Spell to Protect the Hearth

Items required: five small elder or rowan twigs, about 4–5cm (1½–2 inches) long, string or red thread and ribbon
Timing: when the moon is full

The traditional hearth and chimney was considered a portal through which negative energies could enter. Therefore, it was always protected with magic. Go to a place where elder grows and look on the ground for a fallen twig. If there are none, ask the tree's permission before you cut a small length of thin twig, ensuring that it is long enough to cut into the five pieces needed for the spell. Take the twigs home and let them dry out, then on the full moon use them to create a pentacle or five-pointed star. Tie the twigs securely at each point with the string or thread, then loop the ribbon through the top point and hang it from the mantelpiece. The elder is a sacred tree of protection, and the elder star will protect your hearthside from bad vibes.

Blessing to Ward Doors and Windows

Items required: a stick of incense
Timing: daily, ideally each evening before you go to bed

Windows and doors are also portals through which negative energies can enter from the street. They are how most intruders enter the home too, so make sure you have locks in place and never leave windows open when you are not at home. Use this daily blessing to protect these portals from all harm entering your home. Cast it each night about an hour before you go to bed, to protect your home for the next 24 hours and keep the magic strong. Perform the spell while inside the house, to protect those within from all without. Light the incense and, starting at the main door to your home, use the smoke to draw a pentagram across the door, saying:

Keep safe this house, protected be
None shall cross this boundary
Keep safe this house, a welcome place
To those invited to this space

Move around the house in a clockwise direction, repeating the process at every external door and window, on all floors, then place the incense in a holder to burn out. Repeat daily.

Silent Triple-Goddess Blessing for a Harmonious Home

Items required: a small paintbrush, silver paint or moonflower oil
Timing: new to full moon

Lots of witches' homes have hand-painted artwork, sigils, and symbols on the walls and doors, and for this spell you are going to invoke the blessings of the Triple Goddess by decorating your home with her symbol. Don't worry if you don't have permission to paint, or if you need to keep your interest in magic a secret—you can substitute the silver paint for moonflower oil instead, which should dry invisibly. Decide where you want to paint the sigil. You could draw it at the top of the front door, over the mantelpiece, on a headboard, along beams, banisters, kitchen cupboards etc. Once you have decided on the area you wish to charm, use the silver paint or oil to paint the shape of the Triple Goddess symbol, imagining a silver-white light surrounding your home and blessing it with love, joy, and harmony. Allow the paint to dry or the oil to fade and know that you

have used the creative arts to imbue some magic into your house. You can repeat this spell in any room or use other symbols, such as power animals or runes, to give your home a magical ambience. And be prepared to explain the symbols to visitors! As an alternative, you can purchase magical symbols as window decals that peel on and off easily, which would work just as well and can quickly be removed and reused.

A Magical House-Cleansing Ritual

Items required: a besom or broomstick, a mop and bucket, cleaning cloths, three lemons (sliced), hot water, eucalyptus essential oil
Timing: twice a year, at spring and autumn equinoxes or whenever your home feels a little heavy and stagnant

Magical cleansings are performed to imbue the home with fresh and vibrant energies. In this instance, we are using lemon and eucalyptus, as they can help rid the house of stagnant energy or bad vibes. Performing a cleansing like this one can be useful after a period of unrest or disagreement. First, clean the house top to bottom as you normally would. Open all the windows to let fresh air circulate. Then ritually sweep the house using the besom or broomstick—don't actually touch the

A Quick Cleansing Ritual

Items required: a sage smudge stick, an ashtray or small heat-proof bowl, a feather or your hand

Timing: use to dispel a negative atmosphere after an argument, illness, bereavement, or bad news

Sometimes you might need a quick boost to the energy of your home. If you don't have time to perform a full cleansing ritual like the one above, then sage is your best friend. It is renowned for its power to fill an area with positive energy and has been used for centuries by Native Americans. Sage is a natural cleanser, the smoke is quite pleasant, and smudge bundles are inexpensive—or you can make your own by drying a bundle of home-grown sage. To clear your space of bad vibes, light the smudge stick and go all around your home, ensuring that you waft the smoke into every corner of every room. Once you have smudged the whole house, extinguish the sage and allow it to cool before you put it away for next time.

floor, just sweep up all that negative energy, moving around the home in a counterclockwise direction and keeping the broom about 1" above the floor. Take all that bad energy to the door and sweep it out of the house, saying *Begone and don't return!* Next, fill the bucket with hot water and add the sliced lemons and ten drops of eucalyptus oil. Go around the home and use the water to wash down the doors, windows and touch points, again moving in a counterclockwise direction. Then, finally, mop the floors. Use what is left of the water to sprinkle along garden paths, or make up a new batch and wash the doors and windows on the outside too. Drain the water and place the lemons in the compost. Now sit down and rest, because you've earned it!

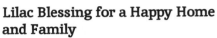

Lilac Blessing for a Happy Home and Family

Items required: a stem of lilac or lilac essential oil, spring water, sea salt, a chalice
Timing: on the new moon

To bring blessings on your home and family, call on the powers of lilac. Lilac is associated with fun, joy, happiness, and the energies of late spring and early summer when it blooms. It is a cheery bloom filled with positive energies. Pour the spring water into your chalice and add a pinch of sea salt. Swirl the chalice to help the salt dissolve, then add the essential oil if you wish to use it. Dip the lilac flower into the water and flick it around the house as you say:

> *Lilac bloom of springtime power*
> *Fill this house with joy*
> *Bring peace and happiness through*
>   *this flower*
> *And a harmony we all enjoy*

Kitchen Witch Household Guardian

Items required: a small statue or picture of a witch that you find pleasing, salt, dried sage
Timing: best performed around Halloween/ Samhain, October 31st

Most magical homes have a household guardian. In this instance we are using a statue of a witch, but you can use something else if you prefer. Traditionally, a small witch was kept in the kitchen to oversee the domesticity that went on there. These statues came to be known as kitchen witches, and they were said to bring good luck. You can still find kitchen witches for sale online and in some New Age shops. Samhain, otherwise known as Halloween, is an excellent time to find one. Once you have found your witch, take her into the kitchen and put her on a plate, then surround her with a circle of salt and sage. Hold your hands over her and say:

> *A kitchen witch here resides*
> *Her magic strong, no need to hide*
> *All who come here feel her power*
> *For she guards and protects us from*
>   *this hour*

Leave the witch in place for 24 hours, then find a home for her somewhere in the kitchen, where she can oversee everything. Scatter the salt and sage to the four winds, giving thanks.

Aloe Vera to Heal Minor Burns

Items required: a potted aloe vera plant
Timing: keep it in the kitchen at all times

Aloe vera is a natural remedy for minor burns, so it's a good idea to keep a plant in your kitchen. It is sometimes referred to as the burn plant for this very reason.

To use it, cut away two or three of the thickest leaves, which tend to grow on the outer edge of the plant. Peel away the outside of the leaf to expose the soft gel inside. Apply the gel to the burn and gently rub into the skin. It has a cooling effect, which offers immediate relief, and the medicinal properties of the plant make the burn heal faster. It is not to be used on severe burns, however, so if the burn site is deep, or covers an area larger than 3" across, seek medical advice. You should never put butter or oil on any kind of burn.

Silent Eucalyptus Ritual for a Sacred Shower

Items required: a stem of fresh eucalyptus
Timing: new to full moon

The bathroom is where you begin and end the day, so it needs to be a welcoming place. Showering off the day before bed is a sacred time of self-care. It helps your mind move from work time into home and family time, and it can help you get a good night's sleep. To give your bathroom a more magical spa-like atmosphere, hang a branch of fresh eucalyptus in the shower, where the steam will release its calming scent. As you shower, imagine the psychic grime of the day washing away and going down the drain. Breathe in the rejuvenating scent of eucalyptus and know that you are safe at home and that it's time to switch off and relax.

And So to Bed Blessing

Items required: *a small blue pouch, amethyst, blue lace agate and sodalite crystals, a teaspoon of dried lavender flowers, an altar pentacle*
Timing: *on the full moon*

Your bed should be a welcome retreat at the end of a long day, and this little pouch of crystals and lavender will help you get a restful night's sleep. Place all the items to charge on the pentacle for a full lunar phase, then place the crystals and the lavender in the pouch. Hang it from the bedpost or place it beneath the mattress to bring about restful sleep.

Blessing for Sweet Dreams

Items required: *lavender sleep spray*

Timing: *perform each time you change the bed sheets*

If you or your child has been having a run of bad dreams, then start to include this blessing as part of your household chores. First, change the bed sheets, and as you put on the clean bedding, spray it generously with the lavender sleep spray, inside and out. Give every part of the bedding a spray, so that the fragrance envelops the sleeper when they get into bed. You can also use lavender-scented ironing water to the same effect. As you spritz the bed, say the following incantation:

> *Lavender let the dreams be sweet*
> *For all who lie within these sheets*
> *I cast this spell with love and charm*
> *To keep the sleeper safe from harm*
> *So mote it be*

As you finish making the bed, pat the pillow three times saying, *Rest, Recharge, Restore.* Hang a dream catcher close by for additional protection against nightmares.

Pins and Needles Spell to Keep Away Unwanted Visitors

Items required: *an external doormat, two sewing pins or needles*
Timing: *on the night of the dark moon*

It can be annoying when your precious time at home is disturbed by salespeople, canvassers and other nuisances, so try this spell to deter unwanted visitors. Take an extra-thick external door mat and, on the underside, weave two sewing pins or needles through the fabric so they form the shape of a St Andrew's cross and remain in place. Ensure that the sharp points of the pins or needles are facing away from your home and out into the street or the hallway of the apartment building. Put the mat in front of the main door to your home and, as you place it down, say,

*Those I do not wish to see, banished,
banished, banished be!*

Fire Spell to Move to a New Home
Items required: a notepad and pen, an idea or image of where you want to move, your cauldron, lighter, dried basil

If you want to move to a new home but don't seem to be getting anywhere, try this spell. Fire spells are a great way to remove blocks. First, write down the reasons why you wish to move, and what you're looking for in your new home. Picture the area or house you want to move to clearly in your mind. Hold that visualization and see yourself there, unpacking boxes and directing the movers with your furniture.

Once you can see this plainly in your mind, roll up the piece of paper, light the end, and drop it in the cauldron to burn. Finally add a pinch of dried basil to the flames and say:

*I wish to move, I will not stay
A new home comes to me this day
A dream now burns for which I long
Basil moves all things along
It brings to me that which I desire
As I move on to a new hearth fire*

CHAPTER ELEVEN

CASTING FOR LOVE AND ROMANCE

Witches are often asked to perform magic on behalf of other people, with prosperity magic and love spells being the most frequently requested. While it is possible for a witch to cast a spell for you, it will never be as effective as the spells you cast for yourself. That's because the witch simply does not have the same emotional investment in the outcome that you do, and your emotions are crucial to effective casting. This is especially true when it comes to love spells.

Love magic is particularly dependent on emotions, because there is no greater feeling than that of love. Love is amazing, exhilarating, confusing, infuriating, and frustrating. At times, it can be a lonely experience too. It is nevertheless a road that we must all navigate, often more than once, so having magic on your side can be a good thing. It all begins, however, with love for yourself.

SELF-LOVE IS KEY

We live in a world where comparison is rife. Social media means that we are constantly bombarded with images of other people, their lifestyle, their clothes, even the food they eat and the places they go. All of this can have a negative impact on your self-esteem if you let it. Remember that social media is a highlight reel, and the people you follow will have dark days and low moods, just as you do.

The impact of all this comparison is that people often find it challenging to love themselves or think of themselves as worthy. Instead, they fall into the trap of feeling as if they aren't good enough, rich enough, pretty enough, or *anything* enough for the modern world. But for someone else to love you, you have to love yourself first. Why? Because bolstering someone else's self-esteem can be exhausting. People are reluctant to attach themselves to someone who is needy, clingy, or dependent on them for feelings of self-worth. They are more likely to be charmed by someone who is in a good place mentally and who enjoys their own company. So your best chance at love is to learn to love yourself first.

Blessing for Self-Love

Items required: a pink candle and holder, a pink ribbon, a ring that is special to you
Timing: at the time of the new moon

When the first sliver of a new moon is visible in the sky, go to a quiet place. Light the pink candle and focus on the flame. Then thread the ring onto the pink ribbon and twirl it around the candle flame in a clockwise direction, following the path of the sun. As you do so, chant the words:

I am worthy of love, from myself and others

Continue for as long as you like, then blow out the candle. Repeat each night until the moon is full or the candle has burnt away.

Silent Ritual Charm for Self-Love

Items required: a small spell jar and stopper, rose incense stick and holder, a small slip of paper and a pen, a lock of your hair, three rose quartz shards, three dried rose petals, pink Himalayan salt, a pink candle or sealing wax, a pentacle
Timing: at the time of the full moon

To begin with, cleanse the spell jar using the smoke from the rose incense, then place the incense in a holder to burn throughout the ritual. Write your name and date of birth on the slip of paper, roll it around the lock of hair and put it into the spell jar. Add the three rose petals and the three rose quartz shards. Fill the jar with the pink salt, put on the stopper, and seal it with pink wax. Leave the spell jar in place on the pentacle until the following full moon, then place it by your bed or on your dresser to exude its magic.

ATTRACTING LOVE

There are some things we can't control, but our appearance and how we present ourselves to the world *isn't* one of them. Self-love also involves making the best of your appearance, so prepare for each day as if you are going to meet it head on. Then cast the following spells to enhance your allure and attract love.

Three-Moons Spell to Attract Love

Items required: three red candles, half a teaspoon of blessing seeds, mortar and pestle, paper towels, rose or lavender oil, an athame or carving tool, a cauldron or heat-proof bowl, a lighter
Timing: on the full moon, three months in a row

Take one of the candles and carve what you are hoping to attract into the length of the wax: Love, Romance, New Boyfriend/Girlfriend etc. Put half a teaspoon of blessing seeds, also known as nigella seeds, into the mortar and grind to a powder with the pestle. Empty the powder onto a paper towel, anoint the candle in the oil, then roll it through the blessing-seed powder, pulling the candle toward you to bring love into your life as you say:

> *A lover comes by candle's glow*
> *From where or when I do not know*
> *They come to me, true love to share*
> *As the smokes curls through the air*
> *As this wax melts, so do our hearts*
> *Together a new life we start*
> *And by the burning of this flame*
> *Within three/two/one moons I will*
> *   know their name*
> *So mote it be*

Melt the bottom of the candle and set it in the cauldron. Light the wick and allow it to burn down completely. Repeat with the next candle on the next full moon, adapting the final line of the incantation so that you are counting down the moons until your lover appears.

Love Witch Spell

Items required: a king or queen of hearts playing card, rose oil or water, a magnet
Timing: on the new moon

If you want to bring more love into your life, use this spell to become a love magnet! On the night of the new moon, take the items to a quiet place where you will not be disturbed. Take the playing card and anoint the four corners, front and back, with rose oil or rose water, then gently brush the magnet across the image of the king or queen, beginning at the crown and moving toward the chest of the image. As you do so, chant the words:

Like the king/queen of hearts, I am a magnet to love

Continue until you feel the magic *pop*, then place the playing card in your bag or wallet and carry it with you at all times. You should notice that you attract more romantic attention in the coming weeks and months.

Silent Charm for Luck in Love
Items required: red or pink sealing wax, baking parchment, ground cinnamon powder, a seal that represents love—a heart, rose or cupid—or a carving tool

Heat the sealing wax until it forms a large pool on the parchment, add a sprinkling of cinnamon to bring good luck and blessings toward you, then apply the seal to the cooling wax to create an image. If you do not have a romantic seal, use your carving tool once the wax has cooled, and carve a heart into the wax. Once the wax has hardened, peel off the paper and carry the charm with you.

White Rose Spell to Determine Someone's True Intentions
Items required: a single white rose, a white ribbon, a bud vase and water, a slip of paper, a red pen
Timing: at the new moon

Not everyone who flirts with you will have positive or good intentions. The white rose is a symbol of purity, and can be used to determine if your lover's intentions are honorable. Write their name on the slip of paper in red ink. Use the ribbon to tie the name tag on to the stem of the rose. Hold your hands over the rose and say:

A nagging doubt is in my mind so I must test their will
Their true intentions I would find, be they good or ill
Rose of love and purity, now tell all with your charm

Is this lover true to me, or do they mean me harm?

Place the rose in a bud vase of water and care for it well. If it blooms and opens wide, your lover's intentions toward you are pure and kind. If, however, the rose fails to open fully, then wilts and dies, they are holding secrets from you and their intentions are questionable. Let the rose be your guide.

Spell to Bring Love to Your Door

Items required: three red or pink roses
Timing: best performed at sunset, during a waxing moon

Pull the petals from three red or pink roses and put them in a pocket, pouch, or bowl. Go outside and walk away from your house, enjoying the sunset and imagining sharing the view with a lover. Once you are some way from your home, turn around and begin to walk back. Chant the following words, out loud or in your head:

Love will come knocking and I will answer

As you walk, scatter the rose petals so that they form a trail to your door, but do not use them all. Keep a few aside and place them in a pouch or dish by your bed. Love should come knocking within a full lunar phase.

Apple Spell to Deepen Bonds of Love

Items required: at least one apple (more if you choose the pie option), a sharp knife, cinnamon and nutmeg
Timing: best performed during a waxing moon, or on a special anniversary

Tradition states that to share an apple with your partner will help to deepen the bonds of love between you, and there are two ways that you can use this magic. For a simple charm, cut an apple in half horizontally through the core to expose the seed pentacle in the middle, sprinkle it with cinnamon and nutmeg for a fruitful union, then give one half to your lover and eat the other half yourself. Alternatively, you can bake the magic into an apple pie by following a basic recipe and adding a generous sprinkling of spices to the apples

sure that all the seeds are in a row, at the same height. Each suitor is now represented with a seed that bears his or her initial. Finally, light the wick of the candle. As the candle burns, the seeds should fall, but the seed that sticks the longest is the suitor you should choose, as he or she is the type to stick around.

Spell to Heal a Rift Between Lovers

Items required: an empty jar and lid, a jar of runny honey, pink paper, scissors, a pen, pink or red sealing wax
Timing: during the waning moon

Relationships can be difficult, and you won't always see eye to eye with your partner. If an argument has left an atmosphere of discord between you, cast this spell to help heal the rift. Cut two hearts from the pink paper. Write your name on one heart and your lover's name on the other. Hold your hands over the hearts and visualize the rift healing. Imagine enjoying happy, romantic times with your partner again. Drop both hearts into the empty jar, then add enough honey to cover them, surrounding the couple in sweetness as you say:

I am sweet to you, you are sweet to me
Together we restore harmony
Heart to heart our spirits lift
By sweetest spell we heal this rift

just before you cover them in pastry. For added magic, top the pie with the initials of you and your lover in pastry, then share the pie as part of a romantic dinner.

Silent Seed Spell to Choose Between Suitors

Items required: a pink, white or cream pillar candle, three (or however many suitors you have) pumpkin seeds, a black felt-tip pen, a lighter
Timing: on the full to waning moon

If you are a flower to bees (lucky you!) and you are having difficulty choosing between suitors, then use this simple spell. Write the initial of each suitor on a pumpkin seed with the black pen. Then heat up the side of the candle with the lighter so that you can stick the seeds to the candle. Make

Seal the spell jar with the sealing wax and keep it in the bedroom. Remember that to move forward, you must let go of the past.

Two-Hearts Spell for Long-Distance Love

Items required: two heart-shaped pebbles, stones or crystals, a pentacle, a chalice of wine or juice
Timing: each full moon

There are many reasons why you could suddenly find yourself in a long-distance relationship, but the most common one is work commitments. If you or your partner have to work away from home for a while, it can be tough to keep the bond strong.

So how do you ensure that your love survives such a situation? Well, you need to find things that forge a bond across the distance, things you can appreciate and that remind you of one another, no matter where you are. The moon is an obvious choice, for its light is reflected the world over. Make a pact with your partner that you will think of each other whenever you see a full moon, and send blessings their way. Then enhance this sentiment by placing the two heart pebbles on the pentacle in the moonlight, toast the moon with the chalice and say:

I drink to you, my lover true
No matter where thou be
I drink to the moon and ask this boon
To send my lover safe home to me

Send your love to your partner, using the moon as your messenger, and finish the wine or juice. Leave the two hearts side by side until the moon begins to wane, then repeat the spell each full moon.

WHEN LOVE TURNS BAD

Occasionally a relationship will fade and deteriorate. When this happens, the pain can be acute as you are forced to say goodbye not only to your partner but also to the life you lived and the future you planned. People come into our lives for a reason, a season or, if we are very lucky, a lifetime. But there are no guarantees.

If you are nursing a heartache, use these spells to help you cope.

Fly-by-Night Spell

Items required: a notepad and pen, sage essential oil, a cauldron, twigs to make a small fire
Timing: on the waning moon, outdoors

If you have discovered that your lover has deceived you or let you down, use this spell to clear them from your life. We think of a *fly-by-night* as someone who is only around for what they can get and has no real intentions of sticking around for a committed relationship. Whatever their transgression is, this spell will help you clear their energy from your life so that you can move on.

First, write a letter to your ex-partner explaining how they have made you feel. Tell them about your confusion and resentment. Don't worry, you are never going to send this letter! Just get all your feelings, hurt, and anger down on paper. Next, make a small fire in the cauldron using the twigs. Anoint the letter with the sage oil to cleanse this fly-by-night individual from your life, then fold the letter into the shape of a paper airplane. Hold the plane to your heart and say:

Fly-by-night, leave my sight
Never to return
You had your chance, but by
*   happenstance*
The truth I had to learn
The love I felt now must wither
It fades within my heart
You let me down so go from hither
I am glad that you depart!

As you say the last line of the incantation, throw the paper airplane into the fire and watch it crash and burn.

Spell to Heal a Broken Heart

Items required: a heart-shaped stone or crystal, tissues
Timing: from full to dark moon

*Take all my heart's trouble deep into
    your glen
Lighten my load, that I might love
    again.*

When the heart is safely buried, walk away from the site and do not look back.

If you have had your heart broken, try this little spell to kick-start the healing process. Hold the pebble to your heart as you think about the circumstances of the heartbreak. If tears bubble up, wipe them with a tissue. When you are ready, kiss the stone and wrap it in the tissue as you say:

*I wrap my heart in tears so that I can
    release the sorrow it holds*

Next, go for a walk, taking the stone with you. Try to find a crossroads where three or four paths meet and bury the stone there. Next, say:

*Earth heals my heart which is heavy
    and sore
Let healing begin, that it bleeds no
    more*

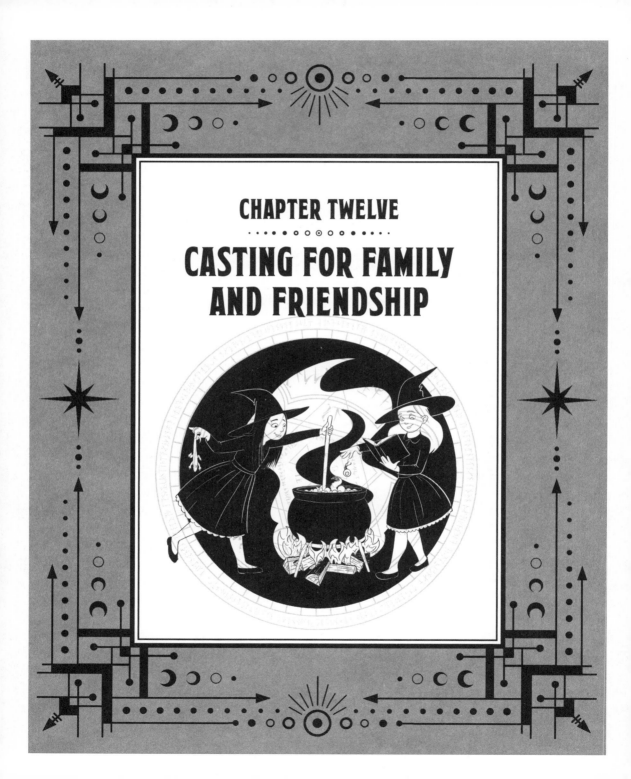

CHAPTER TWELVE

CASTING FOR FAMILY AND FRIENDSHIP

While you can choose your friends and the company you keep, family is a different matter. It is a unit made up of many personalities, so there are bound to be clashes now and then. Family dynamics also change over the years, as siblings grow up, leave home, get married and have kids, as parents age and grandparents pass away. A family is an ever-changing entity, growing and expanding with new generations but shrinking and adapting with the losses too.

The family is our first experience of society. And in any family there are universal issues that come up time and again, such as sibling rivalry and jealousy, the black sheep who turns away from the flock and strikes out alone, the covert competitiveness, the needy/naughty sibling who takes up all the attention, the controlling parent who just won't let go, and so on.

It's a minefield, to say the least. Fortunately, this chapter has some spells and rituals to help make your interactions with family and friends run as smoothly as possible.

DEFINING FAMILY

The people you feel closest to and spend the most time with are your family. These people might not be blood relatives; they might be step-relatives, work colleagues you get along especially well with, or friends. Some magical people who take part in a coven might also consider the coven to be their magical family. So the word *family* has a different meaning to different people. Whatever works for you is okay, so don't feel that this chapter is irrelevant to you if you don't have a traditionally defined family. Simply adapt the spells to suit the kind of family you do have, and go from there.

DINNER'S ON THE TABLE!

Have you ever wondered why your parents may have insisted that you all gather around the table at dinner time, or why Sunday dinner took place at your grandparents' house every week? It's because sharing food is a primal form of bonding. Sharing meals as a family creates a stronger bond between individuals, and that cannot be understated when it comes to family.

Blessing for a Family Meal
Items required: prepare a meal for your family
Timing: as often as possible

Arrange a lovely home-cooked meal with your family members. It need not be anything elaborate, something simple will suffice, so if you prefer a barbecue, tacos or afternoon tea to Sunday dinner with all the trimmings, then go with that. As you

prepare the meal, think back on all the times you have enjoyed good food with your family, and express gratitude that they are in your life. Then say:

> *The food we share shows that we care*
> *And that our bond is true*
> *As we eat this meal, the love we feel*
> *Is strengthened and renewed*
> *So mote it be*

Enjoy the meal with your family and friends and know that you have partaken in an ancient form of magical bonding. If you don't enjoy cooking, make a reservation at a nice restaurant and say the incantation just before you leave the house.

SIBLING RIVALRY AND FRENEMIES

The people you grew up with will always have the ability to push your buttons, because they probably know you inside out. They have been privy to your past moments of embarrassment, and may know who your first kiss was with or how you got that scar on your left knee. For many people that amounts to no more than teasing in adulthood, but for some it becomes a source of bitter divide.

While a certain amount of competition is healthy between siblings, if it goes too far it can become damaging. The same is true when it comes to friends. There may be times when a friend can seem more like an enemy. If you are dealing with a friend who has demonstrated enmity toward you on occasion, it might be best to leave them behind, especially if you have confronted them over their spite before and their behavior toward you has not improved.

You may use this spell to try and restore a sense of peace between you and a friend or sibling.

Spell for Easing Sibling Rivalry
Items required: your toothbrush, your sibling's toothbrush, a pink ribbon
Timing: on the full moon

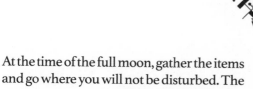

At the time of the full moon, gather the items and go where you will not be disturbed. The toothbrushes act as a tag lock because they are something you use every and they are imbued with your energies. Pick up your toothbrush and name it after yourself, then do the same with the other toothbrush, naming it after your sibling. Place the toothbrushes side by side on top of the ribbon. Hold your hands over them and say:

This sibling bond now turned sour
Will begin to repair from this hour
I am here for you, you are there
*   for me*
Together we are a family
From this day forth and by this spell
We learn to wish each other well

Finish the spell by tying the ribbon in a bow and securing the two toothbrushes together. Keep them hidden and do not untie them until the sibling bond has strengthened between you.

Spell to End a Toxic Friendship

Items required: one lemon, salt, two pins, an athame or sharp knife
Timing: on the waning moon

If a friendship has turned irretrievably sour, it is in your interests to end it. There is no point wasting time and energy on someone who is working or speaking against you, or who has proven they don't deserve to be in your life. Lemon and salt are both natural cleansers, and this spell uses both to cleanse the toxic friend from your life.

Hold the lemon as you think of your ex-friend. Cut partway through the lemon in an X shape. Gently pull the lemon open to reveal the citrus flesh inside and pour salt into the fruit as you say:

I cleanse toxic friendships from
*   my life*
I do not need the trouble and strife
Go from me and get thee gone
By this magic be it done!

Push the lemon together and secure with the two pins, crossing them in an X shape, like crossed swords. Leave the

between family members is positive in nature. Hold the tube of toothpaste in your hands and say:

> *I turn to you, you turn to me*
> *We unburden our hearts freely*
> *We speak our minds, get things off our*
>   *chest*
> *In love and trust we are blessed*
> *This paste keeps communication clear*
> *For within this house there is naught*
>   *to fear*
> *Blessed be*

lemon on your altar for three days, then remove the pins and put the salted lemon in the compost. As the fruit rots away, the friendship will fade.

Spell for Communication

Items required: the family toothpaste
Timing: charge and empower at the time of the new moon

Empowering an everyday object with magical intent is one of the easiest ways to create positive magic. Family harmony depends largely on how well you communicate with one another, and you should all be able to express your feelings in a kind and considerate manner. Since everyone uses toothpaste, this little charm will help ensure that the communication

Repeat this charm with each new tube of toothpaste. If communication has been especially difficult, or if you come from a family where toxic interactions are a regular occurrence, you might need to cast this spell several times before you begin to see the positive effects. Don't give up! Remember that all magic has an effect, but it isn't instantaneous. For extra power, work this spell in combination with the one below.

Lavender Scones Spell for Family Harmony

Items required: ingredients for scones, half a teaspoon of lavender, cream, jam or honey, a pentacle
Timing: whenever your family get together

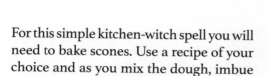

For this simple kitchen-witch spell you will need to bake scones. Use a recipe of your choice and as you mix the dough, imbue it with your magical intention by saying:

Lavender's blue, lavender's sweet
Harmony comes through this treat

Stir in the lavender as you mix the dough, then bake the scones. Serve them with cream and honey or jam, using the altar pentacle as a serving platter and offering the scones to each member of the family.

Silent Spell to Spread a Little Loving Energy

Items required: an empty spray bottle, spring water, rose and lavender essential oil
Timing: make the potion on a new moon

Scents are one of the quickest ways to create an atmosphere of comfort and safety. With this simple potion, you can create an atmosphere of loving energy using the natural properties of essential oils. First fill the spray bottle with pure spring water, then add ten drops each of lavender and rose essential oil. Screw on the top and shake to disperse the oils, then spray liberally throughout the room you spend the most time in as a family. Use this potion whenever your family needs an extra boost of love.

Spell to Call in a Black Sheep

Items required: a spool of black thread, an empty toilet-paper tube, scissors, a small picture of the relative you want to connect with, glue
Timing: begin at dark moon

Occasionally, family dynamics can be so stifling to some people that they feel the need to break free and go it alone. They might cut themselves off altogether. This autonomy and free will should be respected, but there may also be times when you need to contact and reconnect with them, and that is where this spell comes in. Keep in mind, however, that it may not lead to a lasting reconciliation, although it should at least bring about a reunion. The decision as to whether they re-join the family permanently is up to them.

Begin this spell when the moon is dark. It will take several days to complete and must be worked daily. First, glue the picture of the black sheep onto the cardboard tube. Next cut a small nick in one end of the tube and use it to secure the end of the black thread. To perform the spell, turn the tube three times, using it to reel in the thread from the spool. As you do so, say:

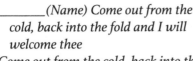

_____(Name) *Come out from the*
cold, back into the fold and I will
welcome thee
Come out from the cold, back into the
fold and complete our family

Do this each day, reeling in the thread by three turns a day until the spool is empty and the tube is full. Seal the end of the thread in place with a little wax. You should hear news of the black sheep within three moons.

Silent Spell to Hear from an Old Friend

Items required: a piece of pink paper and a red pen, a pink birthday candle, a citrine crystal
Timing: on the new moon

If there is an old friend you've lost touch with and would like to hear from, then cast this spell. Write their name seven times in a column on the pink paper, using the red pen. Then, from the top, fold the paper toward you seven times, folding in each name as you go. Think of your friend as you do this. Light the pink birthday candle and seal the folded paper with the wax, then blow out the candle with a wish to hear from your friend. Place the paper and the citrine crystal, which represents communication, by the

phone. Repeat the wish every day until the birthday candle has burned down. You should hear news of your friend within one lunar cycle.

Silent Poppet Spell to Strengthen Family Bonds

Items required: paper, a pen, glue or tape
Timing: new to full moon

Use poppet magic to strengthen family bonds. Simply make a chain of paper dolls, ensuring that there are as many dolls as family members. Lay the dolls out in row and name each one for a relative by writing their name on a doll. Finally, place the dolls in a circle, with the names facing inward, and secure the hands of the two end dolls with the glue or tape. These poppets now represent the family circle, so keep them somewhere safe. This is a lovely spell to do with small children, because you can get them to paint the poppets to represent each member of the family.

ONE OF THE FAMILY

Families expand to include new members, usually due to a marriage or birth. Families also expand when two families are united by marriage or a romantic relationship, leading to step-families, or reconstructed families as they are also known. It isn't always easy to adjust, and it can take time

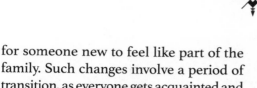

for someone new to feel like part of the family. Such changes involve a period of transition, as everyone gets acquainted and eventually settles down together. A simple ritual to welcome a new member of the family can help smooth things along.

Ritual to Welcome a New Family Member

Items required: tea-lights, a wax taper
Timing: on the first full moon following the introduction of the new member

Take as many tea-lights as you have relatives, including yourself and the new member. Hold back one of the tea-lights, place the rest in a circle, and name them for yourself and your relatives as you light them with the taper. Allow them to burn for a short time, then carefully widen the circle of flames to leave a gap. Light the final tea-light, naming it for the new member, and place it in the gap to complete the family circle. Then say:

A kindred spirit comes our way
We welcome him/her in kind
We hope they choose to join and stay
As a welcome place with us they find
Blessed be

Allow the candles to burn out naturally and do all you can to make the new relative feel welcome and accepted.

BABY BLESSINGS

It is customary in many traditions, including magical ones, to bless a newborn in order to protect it until its official naming ceremony. Keys have long been used in magical protection. In the past it was said that placing an iron key beneath the baby's pillow would prevent it from being stolen by fairies and a changeling left in its place. In Yorkshire, England, it is customary to offer keys as baby gifts and to give the baby a piece of jet to ward away bad omens and energy.

Key Blessing for a Newborn

Items required: a baby toy shaped like a key, a piece of jet, a silver coin, a dried rosebud, a pouch
Timing: soon after the baby is born

When you see the baby for the first time, bring the key toy and the pouch into which you have placed the piece of jet crystal, the silver coin and the dried rosebud, thus offering protection, prosperity and love to the baby. Place the pouch into the folds of the baby blanket for a few minutes, then replace it with the key toy. Once you have offered these things to the newborn, take them to the baby's nursery at home, placing the key into the empty crib and hanging the pouch close by. This will ensure a safe space when the child comes home from the hospital.

SAYING GOODBYE

Just as people come into a clan, people leave it too. This is usually due to death, divorce or relocation. Saying goodbye to someone you love is never easy, but families have a remarkable way of adapting and coming together in such difficult times. It is not unusual for a bereavement to be the catalyst that heals a rift, for example, or for some relatives to maintain friendship connections with a sibling's or child's ex-partner. Whatever the circumstances, saying goodbye to a loved one is hard. Use this spell to make the adjustment a little easier.

Ritual to Say Goodbye

Items required: *tea-lights, a wax taper*
Timing: *on the first dark moon following the loss*

You can cast this spell with your family or alone. Take as many tea-lights as you have relatives, including yourself and the person who is leaving. Keeping back one of the tea-lights, place the rest in a circle and name them for yourself and your relatives as you light them. Allow them to burn for a short time, then carefully place the final tea-light in the center of the circle and light it. This candle represents the person who is gone. Allow the candles to burn for a while, then extinguish the tea-light in the center, leaving the others lit, as you say:

> *A soul is gone from us this day*
> *We bid a fond farewell to them*
> *We accept they could not stay*
> *We hold on to our memories and*
>   *cherish them*
> *Blessed be*

Allow the candles to burn out naturally and know that it will take time to process the loss you have suffered, so be kind to yourself and each other.

A Spell for Understanding

Items required: *a small pouch, citrine and rose quartz crystals, a pentacle*
Timing: *new to full moon*

If there is something you want to discuss with a family member and you are nervous about their reaction, cast this simple spell for greater understanding. Place the crystals to charge on the pentacle from new to full moon. When the moon is full, put them in a pouch, hold them, and say:

> *A secret I would share with you*
> *Please try to see my point of view*
> *I will empathize with you*
> *And a new understanding bonds us*
>   *two*

Keep the pouch with you as you speak to your relative. Remember that people need time to process new information, so allow them space if they need it.

Ritual to Draw New Friends

Items required: *none*
Timing: *whenever you see a fallen penny*

To bring new friends into your life, say this charm whenever you see a fallen penny on the ground:

> *See a penny, pick it up*
> *With new friends I soon will sup*
> *As I walk down every street*
> *Each shining penny is a pal I'll meet!*

To Make a Blessing Charm for a Loved One

Items required: *silver or gold sealing wax, baking parchment, blessing seeds*
Timing: *during a waxing moon*

To make a magical good-luck charm for a loved one, heat the sealing wax and pour it onto the paper to form a pool. Add a pinch of blessing seeds while the wax is hot, and say:

> *I cast this blessing from me to thee*
> *That good fortune finds you wherever*
>   *you may be*

Wait for the wax to cool, and once it has hardened, peel off the paper and give the talisman to your loved one, explaining that it is a charm for good luck and they need to carry it with them.

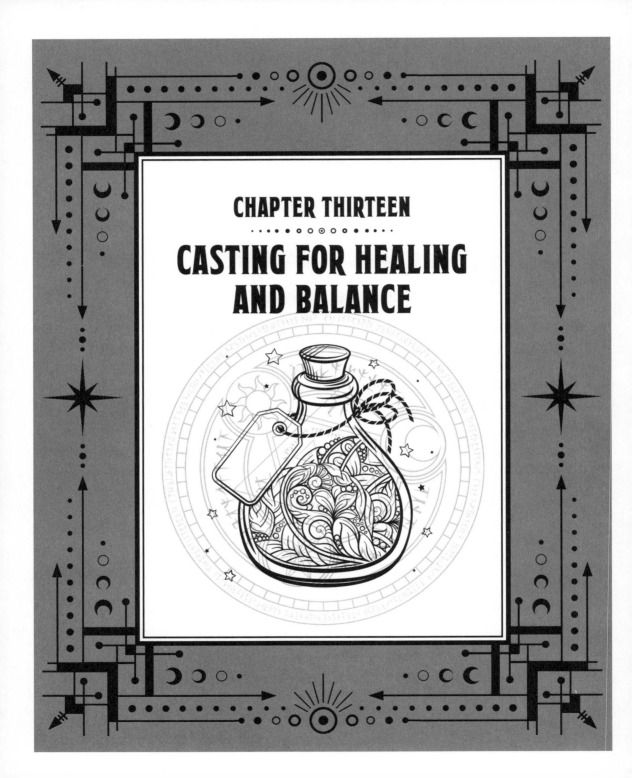

CHAPTER THIRTEEN

CASTING FOR HEALING AND BALANCE

Healing is not the same as curing. Some illnesses can't be cured; others are temporary. Healing is about restoring balance in mind, body, and spirit. In magic, healing is the process of bringing about a sense of equilibrium. While some healing rituals may alleviate the symptoms of illness, others are designed to restore the balance that has been temporarily lost, so a spell to help with symptoms of PMS aims to redress the imbalance brought about by hormones—it doesn't *cure* PMS, it just makes its symptoms easier to bear.

Witchcraft has always been a healing tradition; the wise women of old acted as local doctors and midwives to their neighbors. In the days before antibiotics and vaccinations, people relied heavily on herbal remedies. Being a wise woman during this time was a dangerous business, as many of the plants used medicinally could also have nasty side effects.

Thankfully, these days witches don't need to scour the countryside trying to identify the correct plants for medicinal use. In fact, unless you are trained in plant identification, leave the foraging to the experts and purchase your herbs from supermarkets and herbalists—or grow them yourself.

In addition, you should never claim to be a medical practitioner or to have healed/cured someone. There are laws in place that regulate medicine and medical practice. Unless you are a medical doctor, you are not qualified to offer a diagnosis or to claim that you can cure anyone.

What you *can* do is cast spells to offer strength and positivity to someone who is going through a tough time, and you can use simple alternative practices such as herbal blends, crystal therapy and aromatherapy potions to comfort yourself and others. You can also offer the most traditional of healing rituals, tea and sympathy, because you should never underestimate the power of a listening ear to help someone feel better.

The gentle healing rituals in this chapter make use of herbs, essential oils, and spell ingredients. There are potions for easing menstrual cramps or for boosting the immune system, along with simple ways to ease a headache, calm a toothache and steam a congested chest. In addition, there are spells to send healing energies to someone who is ill or experiencing a trauma, plus rituals to cope with sorrow and grief if someone you love is diagnosed with a terminal illness. Use these spells responsibly, and research herbs or oils before you use them, particularly if you are substituting ingredients or if you are pregnant or trying to conceive.

TISANES, INFUSIONS AND SIMPLES

Many healing potions come in the form of infusions or tisanes. An infusion is made by steeping leaves in boiling water. When you make a cup of tea, you are making an infusion. A tisane is made by steeping other plant ingredients—flowers, roots, shoots, and spices—in hot water. Usually a tisane is a blend of more than one plant, while an infusion is made with a single plant, such as tea leaves, and is also known as a *simple*. Most herbal tisanes do not contain caffeine, so they can be enjoyed before bed. Some tisanes can also be used as restorative bath soaks, by adding them to the water. Lavender and lemon balm, for example, are good for a calming bath, while rose geranium can help ease menstrual pains.

Lemon and Ginger Potion to Strengthen Immunity

Items required: two lemons, fresh ginger, approx. two teaspoons honey, 4 pints of spring water
Timing: make during a new moon

This potion is great for strengthening the immune system and for easing or warding off colds, flus, and bad coughs during the winter. Ideally, you should drink a hot cup of this tisane every morning, especially during the colder months. Pour the spring water into a pan and add ginger (vary the quantity according to your preference). Slice the lemons and add those too. Heat the mixture and, once the potion is hot, add a couple of teaspoons of honey. Simmer for 5 minutes until the aromas fill the air, then strain, cool and pour into a clean glass bottle. Drink a warm cup of this tisane every day. The mixture should be kept in the fridge and is good for two to three days.

Feverfew to Ease a Headache

Items required: one teaspoon of dried peppermint or feverfew leaves, honey, lavender essential oil
Timing: use as soon as you feel the first niggle of a headache

Feverfew or peppermint tea is very good for soothing a headache or the beginning of a migraine. However, feverfew should not be used if pregnant or breastfeeding, nor should you use it if you are taking any medication for thinning blood or for blood pressure, so use peppermint instead. Steep the leaves in hot water for three to four minutes, strain and sip slowly. Rubbing a drop or two of lavender essential oil into your temples can also help reduce the headache, as can lying in a darkened room. Try to avoid stimulants such as caffeine, tobacco, or chocolate, which can exacerbate a headache. Also avoid screens.

Arnica to Bring Out Bruising
Items required: an empty dark glass bottle, arnica essential oil, ¼ fl oz almond oil
Timing: on a waxing moon, if possible

Arnica is a natural anti-inflammatory, so it can ease mild aches, pains, and soreness. Due to its potency, you need to dilute it in a carrier oil first, so add five drops of arnica essential oil to ¼ fl oz of almond oil. Store it in a dark glass bottle, away from sunlight. To ease the pain of bumps and bruises, gently rub a little of the oil onto the affected area. This will help the bruise bloom quickly and heal more rapidly. Apply daily until the bruise is gone or the soreness has eased.

Do not use arnica on broken skin, as it is too strong and can cause irritation.

Rose-Water Compress to Reduce Swelling
Items required: a crepe bandage, rose water or rose essential oil, spring water, a bowl
Timing: use on sprains and swollen joints

Rose makes an excellent base for a cold compress, which can be applied to reduce swelling caused by sprains. Place an unrolled bandage into a large bowl, then add cold spring water to soak the bandage. Next, add two tablespoons of rose water, or 6 drops of rose essential oil. Stir the bandage around in the rose water, then place the bowl and its contents into the fridge for about 10 minutes. Once the bandage has cooled and soaked up the rose water, wring

Let the flowers steep in the oil, shaking the bottle each day. There is no need to strain it; you can leave the flowers in the oil. Apply the potion to the irritated skin. Do not use if pregnant, as calendula can bring on menstruation.

Geranium Massage Oil for Menstrual Discomfort

Items required: an empty dark glass bottle, 1 fl oz almond oil, rose geranium essential oil
Timing: make on the full moon

This gentle message oil can help alleviate the discomfort associated with periods, such as stomach cramps, lower back pain, and breast tenderness. Pour 1 fl oz of almond oil into a clean, dark glass bottle and add six to ten drops of rose geranium oil. Gently massage the oil into the stomach, lower back, and breasts to ease the discomfort. Use as soon as you feel the first twinges of menstrual pain.

it out and apply it to the swollen area, being careful not to wrap the bandage too tightly. If the swelling hasn't reduced with an hour, seek medical attention.

Calendula to Soothe Irritated Skin

Items required: two tablespoons of dried calendula flowers, 1½ fl oz almond or sunflower oil, an empty bottle
Timing: make at the time of the new moon

Calendula is a little golden marigold flower that is frequently added to beauty products. It is a mild astringent and has antifungal properties. It is a gentle way to treat mild skin irritations, mild sunburns, rashes, and blemishes. To make calendula oil, drop two tablespoons of dried calendula flowers into a bottle and add 1½ fl oz of a carrier oil, such as almond, olive, or sunflower.

Raspberry and Sage for Sore Throats

Items required: half a teaspoon of dried raspberry leaves, half a teaspoon of dried sage leaves, honey
Timing: use whenever you have a sore throat

Steep the herbs in boiling water for around five minutes, then strain and add honey to

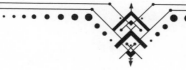

taste. Use this infusion as a gargle to soothe sore throats and tonsillitis.

Spell to Send Strength to a Sick Person

Items required: three pieces of narrow blue ribbon or cord, a lock of the sick person's hair
Timing: on a full moon

Willow trees are known as wishing trees, because it is said that a wish whispered beneath its boughs is sure to be granted. Trees of all kinds are also a great source of strength. This spell calls on the spirit of the willow tree to lend strength to the person who is ill. To begin with, you will need to ask the patient's permission to work a healing spell on their behalf. Once permission is granted, obtain a lock of their hair and plait the three ribbons together, weaving the lock of hair into the plait about halfway down. Secure the braid and then take it with you to a willow tree. Stand beneath the tree, tie the ribbon to a branch, and say:

Willow tree, wishing tree
Send your strength to one dear to me
I tie this braid with hair within
I ask for strength and swift healing
Send your blessing to the one
Who needs it now, so be it done

Give thanks to the spirit of the tree, and walk away when you feel ready, leaving the ribbon in place on the tree.

Charm to Make a Healing Poppet

Items required: blue felt, a needle and thread, a pen and piece of paper, dried herbs for healing—lavender, sage, calendula, chamomile and feverfew, a pentacle
Timing: on the full moon

Write the name of the person you want to send healing energies to on the slip of paper, along with their date of birth. Next, cut two human shapes from the felt and sew them together, but leave the head open. Place the name tag into the poppet first and say _____ (name), I send healing energies your way this day. Fill the poppet with equal amounts of the dried herbs and stitch up the head, then say:

Little poppet I fashioned you from love
I name you for _____
May their illness fade way, may their
*   recovery be swift*
May healing magic pass from you to
*   them, this charm is your gift*
When this work is complete and all is
*   said and done*
I'll cast your herbs onto the earth to
*   once more feel the sun*

them from all sides. Set the anointed candle in a holder and light it. Close your eyes and think of the sick person. Imagine that they are surrounded by a sphere of healing blue light. As you visualize this, chant the following words:

Healed from above, healed from below
Healed from all sides, good health you
  now know
Healed from without, healed from
  within
Healed in all ways, let the healing begin.

Keep the poppet in a safe place. Once the illness has passed, unstitch it and scatter the herbs on the earth. Burn the name tag and the felt poppet, giving thanks.

A Candle Ritual for Healing

Items required: a blue candle and holder, lavender oil, an athame or carving tool, a photo of the person you have permission to cast for
Timing: waxing moon

Place the photo where you can see it as you work. This will be your focus as you cast the spell. Next, carve the name of the person you are sending healing energies to down the length of the candle. Anoint the candle with lavender oil from the top to the middle, and then from the bottom to the middle. This will help draw healing energies to

Continue this chant for as long as you can—you can chant in your head if you want to. Place the candle next to the photograph so its light shines on their face. Let the candle burn down naturally and know that you have sent good energies to your loved one in their hour of need.

Valley of the Shadow Ritual

Items required: small black candle, myrrh essential oil (or frankincense or sandalwood oils)
Timing: on a waning to dark moon

If someone has been diagnosed with a terminal illness, it is cruel and irresponsible to offer false hope. It is one of the hardest things in the world when someone you love is dying and there is nothing you can do to prevent it. Even medical science has its limits, so you should not feel bad that your magic can't work miracles. You might not be able to offer a cure, but you can perform rituals to help smooth the path you and your loved one must take in order to make the journey as gentle as possible for both of you. This ritual is designed to be repeated whenever you need it, but is best performed on a waning moon. Take the black candle and anoint it with essential oil of myrrh. If you can't find myrrh, you can use sandalwood or frankincense oil as a substitute. Anoint the whole candle from top to bottom, then place it in a holder and light the wick as you say:

> I'll walk the shadow-way with you
> I see all that you're going through
> I'll hold your hand 'til it be time
> I'm safe in your heart, you're safe in mine
> Through all the dark days and nights
>   ahead
> My spirit is there, beside your bed
> I'll walk with you 'til we must part
> Spirit to spirit and heart to heart
> Blessed be

Spell to Invoke a Healing Angel

Items required: an angel lapel pin, a pentacle, a tea-light and holder
Timing: whenever you need a little extra healing power

Angels are universally recognized as benevolent guardians and guides. If someone you know needs a little extra healing, then invoking an angel is a good way to ensure that they are comforted, supported and guided as they navigate illness or trauma. For this ritual you will need an angel lapel pin. You are going to give this pin to the person who needs healing, but first you need to empower it to its purpose and invoke angelic energies to go with it. Place the pin in the center of the pentacle to charge. Light the tea-light and call on celestial help with the following invocation:

> Angels of healing from far and wide
> I invoke your assistance, be by my side
> I cast forth this spell to help heal one
>   I love
> I ask for your aid, shine your light
>   from above
> Let your magic be felt through the
>   charm of this pin
> And as you hold _____ (name) in
>   your wings, let the healing begin
> So mote it be

Leave the pin in place to keep charging for 24 hours and allow the candle to burn out. The next time you see your loved one, give them the pin and tell them it is a reminder that they can all on their angels for help.

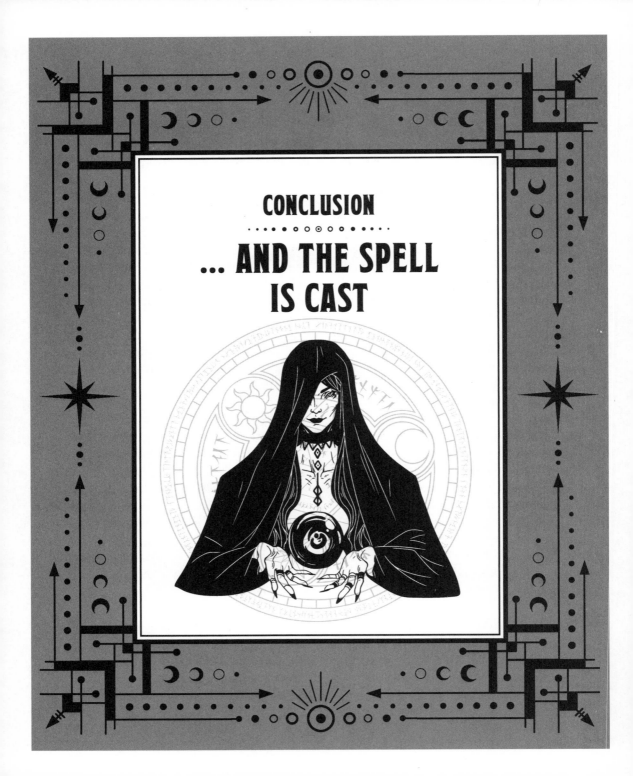

CONCLUSION

... AND THE SPELL IS CAST

I hope you have enjoyed reading this Book of Shadows and Spells, and that you have begun to practice some of the practical magic in its pages. Magic is a natural aspect of life for lots of people, and I trust that you will come to reach for this grimoire time and time again, whenever you need to. My aim has been to show you how simple and accessible magic really is, for those who are brave enough to try it.

You now have at your fingertips all the information you need to live a charmed life, and while some of these spells might appear simple, I encourage you to try them nonetheless, keeping in mind that simplicity is a power in and of itself. This book is designed to be a one-stop shop for all things magical. It is also a jumping-off point, something you can be inspired by when it comes to devising your own spells, rituals, and blessings.

Of the many enchantments in this book, I hope you have found something that is useful to you and has made you feel stronger and more powerful than before, whether that's a piece of psychological information you needed to read or a particular spell you needed to cast. Many of the charms and enchantments here are ones that I have used repeatedly in my own life; I have devised others specifically for this collection. Keep this Book of Shadows close to your heart and it will serve you well. Be bold in your magic, and when life grows dark, reach for these shadows; when you need more light, call on these shadows; and when all is well, celebrate with these blessed shadows. Farewell, my magical reader, until our paths cross again for our next merry meeting. Live magically!

Serene blessings,

Marie Bruce x

FURTHER READING

Buckland, Raymond, *Buckland's Complete Book of Witchcraft* (Llewellyn, 1997)

Cunningham, Scott, *Wicca; A Guide for the Solitary Practitioner* (Llewellyn, 1997)

Cunningham, Scott, *Living Wicca; A Further Guide for the Solitary Practitioner,* (Llewellyn, 1997)

Cunningham, Scott, *The Truth About Witchcraft Today* (Llewellyn, 1997)

Curott, Phyllis, *Book of Shadows* (Piatkus, 1998)

Davis, Owen, *The Oxford Illustrated History of Witchcraft & Magic* (Oxford University Press, 2017)

De Pulford, Nicola, *Spells & Charms* (Godsfield Press, 1999)

Greenleaf, Cerridwen, *The Practical Witch's Spellbook* (Running Press, 2018)

Guiley, Rosemary Ellen, *The Encyclopaedia of Witches and Witchcraft* (Facts on File LTD, 1989)

Horne, Fiona, *Witch; A Magical Journey, A Guide to Modern Witchcraft* (Thorsons HarperCollins, 2000)

Hutton, Ronald, *The Triumph of the Moon; A History of Modern Pagan Witchcraft* (Oxford University Press, 1999)

Illes, Judika, *The Element Encyclopaedia of Witchcraft* (Element HarperCollins, 2005)

Illes, Judika, *The Element Encyclopaedia of 5000 Spells* (Element HarperCollins, 2004)

Kane, Aurora, *Moon Magic* (Quarto Publishing Group, 2020)

Jordan, Michael, *Witches; An Encyclopedia of Paganism and Magic* (Kyle Cathie Limited, 1998)

Moorey, Teresa, *Spells & Rituals* (Hodder & Stoughton, 1999)

Moorey, Teresa, *Witchcraft; A Beginner's Guide* (Hodder & Stoughton, 1996)

Moorey, Teresa, *Witchcraft; A Complete Guide* (Hodder & Stoughton, 2000)

Morningstar, Sally, *The Wicca Pack; Weaving Magic into your Life* (Godsfield Press, 2001)

Morningstar, Sally, *The Wiccan Way* (Godsfield Press, 2003)

Saxena, Jaya & Zimmerman, Jess, *Basic Witches* (Quirk Books, 2017)

Van de Car, Nikki, *Practical Magic* (Running Press, 2017)